MOTHER & I

Ianto Ware is is the author of *Twenty-One Nights in July: A Personal History of the Tour de France* and the long-running zines *Westside Angst* and *Das Papierkrieg*. He was the founding director of Adelaide's Format Festival, producer of the Festival of Unpopular Culture, and CEO of Renew Adelaide. More recently, he was the Co-Director of the National Live Music Office. He lives in Sydney with his partner, the artist Diana Baker Smith, and their son.

MOTHER & I

The history of a wilful family

IANTO WARE

Hunter Publishers
PO Box 6077
Santa Lucia
Queensland, 4067
Australia
www.hunterpublishers.com.au

First published 2021: Hunter Publishers
This edition published 2023

Cover design: Design by Committee
Text design: Anne-Marie Reeves

Cataloguing-in-Publication data is available from National Library of Australia

Ware, Ianto
Mother and I: the history of a wilful family
ISBN 9780648848189 (pbk.)

For my mother, Dimity Ann Ware (28 May 1952 –
16 May 2018), and my grandmother, Shirley Constance Ware,
with thanks, on the occasion of her 90th birthday.

'Motherhood – unmentioned in the histories of conquest and serfdom, wars and treaties, exploration and imperialism – has a history, it has an ideology...'
— Adrienne Rich

1

> Famous men have from time immemorial had their life stories told, and even our generation, with all its stupid indifference to the present, has not quite abandoned the practice. The outstanding personality has still won an occasional triumph over the blind hostility to merit that poisons all states, small and great alike. — Tacitus

When she was twenty-four my mother received a kidney transplant. Her doctors told her she could never have children and would probably die in her thirties. In response, she announced her lesbianism, left my father, and gave birth to me. Contrary to expectations, she lived for a further thirty-eight years, dying just before her sixty-sixth birthday.

I was conceived in May 1979, during her final foray into heterosexuality, in the week before she left my father. Their marriage had become untenable the previous spring when Mother fell in love with a woman for the first time. It was early November and the neighbourhood jacarandas were in bloom. The woman's name was June and she was a hypochondriac, a fact that brought the relationship to its abrupt end shortly after my birth.

Nonetheless, when I arrived, Mother took that Arcadian spring as a sort of origin myth for our small family. Every November throughout my childhood, she would bundle me into the car, along with our dogs, Suzie and Cassie, and we would drive through the suburbs looking for blooming jacarandas.

When we found them, she would pull over, peer up into their purple blossoms, sigh wistfully, and tell me, 'The jacarandas were in bloom when I first fell in love with a woman.' She would pause, 'Her name was June. I left her because she was a hypochondriac.'

After that, she would recount the final days of her marriage, her pregnancy, and the summer of my birth. It was a time in which she had defeated death and created new life.

When I was two, she purchased a house in the suburb of Flinders Park, on the outskirts of Adelaide. It was not a pleasant location. There were no remarkable views or landmarks and, like so many post-war suburbs, it possessed an Orwellian uniformity. Mother was not blind to its faults, and knew she would never fully pay off the mortgage on her meagre income, but she felt I needed a stable sense of home.

A few months earlier she had replaced June with a self-described 'bar dyke' known simply as Rammy, from whom I would inherit a love of the British metal band Motörhead. I was going through a phase in which I refused to wear clothes and spent most of my time naked but for a plastic Spider Man mask. Our neighbours were mostly older conservative heterosexuals who took an immediate dislike to us.

Mother was undeterred. Within months, she began tearing up the lawn, laying down a carpet of manure, and plotting out her future garden. I spent much of my childhood following her through plant supply stores, where she purchased huge quantities of potting soil, shrubs, and ground cover.

One day, while driving in the countryside, we found some acorns, which we planted in the front yard. They dug their way into the alluvial soil and grew with unnatural speed into a grove of mighty oaks. Soon their spires loomed menacingly above Flinders Park, and a mass of greenery pressed up against the fence line. The neighbours viewed us with growing animosity, but by that point Mother had created a forest so dense they were virtually invisible.

Her garden was both intended and received as a wilful act of non-conformity; an unruly incursion of uncontrolled wildness in a landscape otherwise defined by rigid quarter-acre blocks, cream brick houses, and close-trimmed lawns. She was not alone in approaching gardening from this perspective. Indeed, there has been a history of radical gardening just as long as there have been dull suburbs full of people who take their lawns too seriously.

After Mother died, I read William Morris's 1882 essay 'Making the Best of It'. He describes her attitude perfectly:

> Suburban gardeners...wind about their little bit of gravel walk and grass plot in ridiculous imitation of an ugly big garden of the landscape-gardening variety, and then with a strange perversity fill up the spaces with the most formal plants they can get; whereas the merest common-sense should have taught them to lay out their morsel of ground in the simplest way [...] and then to fill up the flower-growing space with things that are free and interesting in their growth, leaving Nature to do the desired complexity.

I don't think she had read the essay itself, although she certainly knew something of Morris and his politics. Once or twice a year, we would join my grandparents on a visit to the collection of his work held in the state art gallery, where we would declare the prints beautiful, the furniture uncomfortable, and then adjourn to the gallery café to eat carrot cake.

Like Morris, my mother would occasionally describe herself as a socialist, but I think she approached her politics much as she approached her gardening. She had little formal training in either, yet knew a good deal about both. As a child, I was aware of her politics, mostly because she regularly spoke of her garden as a form of consciousness raising, inflicted on our unwilling neighbours.

'It reminds them that the world isn't orderly and constrained,' she would tell me, 'and they struggle with that, but it's a very good lesson for them.' It was only when I grew older, and inevitably spent more time outside our front gate, that I came to see her point. There was, I slowly learned, a strange and unspoken commitment to uniformity. I noticed this acutely when I entered my teens and found myself constantly offending other boys. I had no idea what I was doing wrong, yet my classmates regularly assured me I was a faggot who needed his head kicked in.

When I asked Mother for advice, she offered only the simplest explanation. 'It's the patriarchy dear,' she would say, 'you just need to ignore it as best you can, and try to make your own, better world.'

I didn't find this very useful. I spent most of my youth alone in my room listening to maudlin pop music, which Mother found extremely annoying. She was always an optimist and grew more cheerful in old age. No amount of neighbourly disapproval seemed to faze her. She found my angst deeply frustrating, and never ceased telling me to cheer up.

Now, well into my forties, I still tend towards melancholy.

It's hard to tell if this is just how I am, or some by-product of the era in which I grew up. I was born in 1980, the time of Margaret Thatcher and Ronald Reagan. One of its leading intellectuals, Francis Fukuyama, famously called it the 'End of History': the point at which humanity simply accepted it had done the best it could possibly do. Even he didn't sound that happy about it:

> The end of history will be a very sad time. The struggle for recognition, the willingness to risk one's life for a purely abstract goal, the worldwide ideological struggle that called for daring, courage, imagination, and idealism, will be replaced by economic calculation, the endless solving of technical problems, environmental concerns, and the satisfaction of consumer demands.

Mother always thought it was a stupid idea. When I went off on one of my tirades about the political malaise of the modern era, she would roll her eyes. 'For goodness sake,' she would tell me, 'don't be such a defeatist.'

It wasn't so much that she couldn't understand my discontent but, during the spring of 1978, she had tapped some unquenchable wellspring of goodwill. It never left her, even in those final months of her life.

The relationship between a single mother and an only child, is by necessity, close, and in our case I think it was exacerbated by the time and place in which we lived. After she died, I was surprised by how much of her world view remained with me. Inevitably, each spring I stumble across a jacaranda, peer up into its branches, and tell whomever I happen to be with, 'The jacarandas were in bloom when Mother first fell in love with a woman. Her name was June. Mother left her because she was a hypochondriac.'

2

> Male superiority is overwhelming: Perseus, Hercules, David, Achilles, Lancelot, du Guesclin, Bayard, Napoleon – so many men for one Joan of Arc.
> — Simone de Beauvoir

After Mother died, I got a lot of advice, all of it well meant but nearly all of it terrible. The death of a parent provokes a level of empathy that's hard to express, and, as a result, it is usually expressed badly. It's worth remembering this when you're grieving.

The most consoling comment I got was, oddly enough, not particularly consoling at all. I was at a dinner party with Diana, my wife, at which I knew no-one and so ended up sitting next to the host's mother. I suppose someone had mentioned I was mourning, as she brought it up over dessert.

'I was sorry to hear about your mum,' she said.

'Thank you,' I replied.

'I have lots of siblings and children,' she continued, 'whereas you had only your mother.'

'I suppose that's true.'

'I can't imagine how I'd feel if all of my siblings and children died at once. But that's effectively what's happened to you, isn't it? You've lost more than your mother.'

She returned to her tiramisu, and I sat contemplating the point. Like anyone in my situation, I mourned the usual things after Mother died: her character, her conversation, those last years in which she suffered without respite. Yet my would-be consoler was right; I had lost something more than an individual. This other loss, less articulable than the grief of Mother's death, produced its own sensation. It sat heavy with me for several months.

It took strange forms. I developed a paranoia that I'd forgotten something. I would often find myself frantically patting my pockets to check I still had my keys, my wallet, or my phone. I began writing down 'To Do' lists, trying to remember the various things I needed to accomplish each day. On several occasions I wrote, 'Call Mother', and then realised this was no longer something I needed to remember.

I saw a therapist who told me it wasn't uncommon to feel this way. In the early weeks of grief, she explained, the sadness is so intense it almost replaces the presence of the deceased. As the mourning period ends, and you make your way back into the world, you're obliged to admit the deceased no longer exists.

'In your case,' she told me, 'I think it's probably a little more complicated because your family was statistically very unusual.'

'How do you mean?' I asked her.

'Well, have you ever met anyone else from a family like yours?'

I had to admit I had not.

'You've lost the only other person who remembers what it was like to be the only queer family in the suburb. You're worried you'll forget it as well, now she's not around to remind you.'

She was right, but she was not consoling. The weeks and months dragged on. I stopped crying every day, but still felt a constant, nagging sense I had forgotten something dreadfully important. In an attempt to resolve it, I read a number of books and essays on dead and dying mothers, sobbing my way through Simone de Beauvoir's glittering *A Very Easy Death*, Roland Barthes' *Mourning Diary*, and even DH Lawrence's thinly fictionalized *Sons and Lovers*.

Writing on the death of a mother is nearly always visceral in tone, riddled with the emotion of lost origins. I noticed the texts written by men were, more often than not, embarrassingly Oedipal. The night after his mother died, Roland Barthes wrote, 'First wedding night. But first mourning night.' DH Lawrence describes the death of his mother like a scene from Snow White:

> She lay raised on the bed, the sweep of the sheet from her raised feet was like a clean curve of snow, so silent. She lay like a maiden asleep.

I was with my mother when she died, and sat by her body afterwards, but this was not how I felt. She was more than the womb from whom I had emerged.

By contrast, I found a number of books written by men on the deaths of their fathers, all of which paired the sense of loss against a fable of patrilineal inheritance. Men wrote about their fathers as something they carried with them long after the separation of death, whereas mothers were usually described as a point of origin, yearned for but no longer needed.

My favourite was Raymond William's *Borderlands*, with his assertion, 'a father is more than a person, he's in fact a society, the thing you grow up into.' This was how I felt about my mother, but it wasn't how mothers were usually written about. From her, I had inherited a certain view of the world, and it was this I was afraid of forgetting.

After that, I read Tacitus' *Agricola*, the biography of his father-in-law, and the former governor of Roman Britain. He wrote it because he was worried Agricola's memory would be besmirched by his enemies, and ultimately forgotten:

> Many of the great men of old will be drowned in oblivion, their name and fame forgotten. Agricola's story has been told to posterity and by that he will live.

Mother had asked for a 'natural burial', with no headstone or marker. The only cemetery offering this kind of service was down the road from the state's largest garbage dump. It was not a location I would have picked. Each time I visited, I placed pebbles on the grave so I could find it again.

Mother sold her house a few months before she died, thinking she would need the money to pay for aged care. A few weeks after the funeral, it was bulldozed, and replaced by two shabby terrace houses. Night after night, I lay awake thinking of the rich soil she had been so proud of, now drowned beneath concrete pavers and double carports. I pictured the grove of oaks cut down, her garden torn up, and all trace of her scrubbed from the face of Flinders Park.

As Robert Carlyle once put it, 'The history of the world is but the biography of great men' and this is mostly how our histories have been written. The end result is a lot of biographies on Churchill and Napoleon, while the names of people like my mother, Dimity Ann Ware, are doomed to oblivion.

Ideologically this annoys me, but it also gnaws at a more personal level. Your family provides not only a sense of origin but of context; the background to the situation you find yourself in, and the first key to making sense of your place in the world. Considering the influence of his ancestors, Evelyn Waugh once wrote:

> The newspapers, I see, have now taken to the expression 'genes' for what was once described as 'blood'. A happier metaphor perhaps is a game of poker. One is dealt a hand the value of which depends on the combined relationship of its components, not on the sum of its numerals. One can 'stand' on what one is given or discard and draw, not always improving the hand by doing so. Every card, high and low, is in the pack of heredity. No two hands are identical.

By the time of her death, Mother and I held markedly different hands. I had become a middle-aged, middle-class man. She had remained a working-class lesbian. It felt like I not only held a different hand, but was playing an entirely different game.

In my early thirties, I left Adelaide and moved to Sydney and, although we spoke regularly on the telephone, certain things we had previously held in common began to fade. She was entering her sixties and already frail. By contrast, I entered my prime, leaving the doldrums of suburban Adelaide for the bustle of Sydney, where I met Diana and took up a respectable job in the civil service.

Before she grew too ill to travel, Mother visited me in Sydney. With her comfort in mind, I purchased a fold-out bed, and set it up in my study, with a view of the harbour. When I awoke the next morning, I found that she had dragged the bedding onto the living room sofa, kicked over a potted plant, and left behind a trail of sand and used tissues. Our apartment was a third the size of her house and, while she enjoyed the views, she found the place too small and the city too busy. She was quick to point out these faults, explaining the relative advantages of Flinders Park.

Similarly, when I returned to my old childhood home, I found it increasingly run-down, and the neighbourhood bleak and vacant. On one of our first visits, Diana observed that everyone in Adelaide seemed to be either in their houses or in their cars, while the city was otherwise deserted. I thought it was quite a funny comment, but Mother took offence and began a campaign against the bourgeois pomposity of Sydney and those who lived there.

From then on, I mostly visited Mother on my own, staying in the spare room looking out over her fernery. Together, we would walk her dog along the river by our house, just as we had when I was a boy. In her later years, she had a curly coated mixed-breed called Arthur, who she rescued from the local pound. As we walked, she would describe the changes to the neighbourhood that had occurred in my absence. These were uniformly minor: the closure of a hardware store, a new nurse at the local vet, or the presence of a family of swans in a nearby park. I think she enjoyed giving me such detailed updates because I was the only person who understood their significance.

As Mother grew old and weak her garden grew stronger and wilder. Large parts of it become entirely inaccessible. Just before I left for Sydney, one of her neighbour's guinea pigs escaped and took up residence in her backyard. The neighbours themselves were arrested for their role in a minor drug cartel but the guinea pig remained for the better part of two years, sleeping in the shed by night and foraging in the undergrowth by day.

When I was a boy, we both assumed I would someday inherit our house and live there indefinitely. Up until my early twenties, we spoke of it as the place in which I would someday raise my own children. After I moved away we slowly abandoned that belief, although we never discussed it directly. When Mother's health began to fail, she found it a difficult place to live and talked about downsizing, leaving Flinders Park, and moving into a smaller place in a nicer neighbourhood.

We had these conversations on and off for the better part of a decade and they became frustratingly cyclical. Whenever she felt ill, she would call me to say the house had become a burden and she wanted to move somewhere smaller. A week later, having recovered slightly, she would ring me again and announce she had decided to stay.

'I spent the morning watching the birds hopping about in the garden,' she would explain, 'What will happen to them if I leave?'

There was a male blackbird who had lived in her garden for so long he had grown white feathers. Mother knew his entire life story, marked by a series of unfortunate partnerships with mates who either died or abandoned him. Each spring he spent weeks building nests only to have them knocked over by a storm or raided by the neighbourhood cats. Mother threw him scraps, left out birdseed and, on hot days, set out bowls of water.

I saw him the last time I visited, white feathered and hopping through the naked boughs of the apple tree. It was the middle of winter, Mother had been dead a week, and I went back to remove the last of her things before I settled the estate. A month later, my aunt phoned to tell me the new owners had cleared the block. I doubt he would have survived as he was too old to withstand such a change.

3

> The quality of a mother's life – however embattled and unprotected – is her primary bequest to her daughter, because a woman who can believe in herself… is demonstrating to her daughter that these possibilities exist. — Adrienne Rich

Georges Simenon once wrote, 'You never really know a person unless you've known his childhood.' By this standard I knew my mother well. In the days after her death, while packing up her house, I found her diaries, the first beginning sometime around the age of eleven, and the last ending in the weeks before her death. With few exceptions, they contained little she had not told me.

In adulthood she wrote poetry, shopping lists, and plans for the garden, but her early diaries were modelled heavily on *The Diary of Anne Frank*. Within them, I recognised many of the stories she told me when I was growing up. However, she always presented them as part of a cohesive mythology, in which she overcame adversity through force of will and brute optimism. This cohesion was absent in her early writing. I was surprised.

I suppose we always know our parents as they are for ourselves; fully formed and well past the bewilderment of childhood. We rarely see the long stream of thoughts and feelings through which they grew into an adult. In Mother's case, I discovered, she had not always been so certain of herself.

It had taken an effort to become the person I knew.

The opening entries of her first diary contain a series of lists illustrating facets of her personality, each written in an uncharacteristically neat and looping cursive. The first, 'a list of things I like', runs to several pages before concluding, 'I like everything, music (especially pop), animals, boats, eating, cars, doing things, lazing, running, jumping, moving, everything.' In the next entry, she lists her interests:

> Now I will tell you about my interests of which I have many. Mostly I like outdoor things. When I was sick I could not do many of these things. I love hiking. We live near the gully and as often as I can, I go for long walks with the dogs. I like walking best when Spring has just started and everything is new, the sun is shining and I am happy. I like walking after the first rain of the dry season. Or just when the first tadpoles come in the creek or when the mushrooms are coming or when the lilacs are out, in fact at any time.

A subsequent entry details her personal failings. It consists of a single line, 'I wish I could be tidy and a pride to my mother.' Shortly afterwards she abandoned both the neat handwriting and the regular entries.

Her early diaries oscillate between two themes. In the first, she documents the bucolic setting of her childhood home, built by my grandparents, Shirley and Deane, into the side of a hill in the middle of a forest. In these, she outlines the various adventures of her two brothers, Kym and Dane, her younger sister Merridy, and their extensive menagerie of pets.

A second theme runs against this, concentrating on her

fragile health. She contracted kidney disease in early infancy. It got worse as she got older, leading to a near-death experience when she was eleven. She had grown dangerously ill, and her doctors had proposed an experimental operation, for which they expressed very little optimism. My grandparents agreed to it because they thought she would die within a matter of months.

Mother recounted the operation to me on a number of occasions, beginning with her voyage into the surgical theatre, and the sensation of slowly dissolving into an ether, vast and dark. Within this void, she felt no fear; only an immense sense of comfort and warmth. She saw no indication of an afterlife, but knew that she was on the precipice of death. Contemplating the situation, she decided to wake up. When she did so, she found the operation had been a success.

I was usually told this story as a prelude to the fable of June and the jacarandas, imparted as part of an odyssey in which Mother confronted mortality, cast aside the mantle of heterosexuality, and spawned a child. In her telling of it, the decision to live was purely a matter of will, and I grew up thinking she had been indefatigably courageous since childhood.

Her early diaries are less stoic. For much of the time, both before and after the surgery, she was bedridden. She found the experience violently frustrating and became uncharacteristically despondent. To cheer her up, my grandmother gave her books by Rosemary Sutcliff, a well-known writer of children's historical fiction.

Sutcliff had a penchant for writing about children with some sort of disability, having suffered from chronic illness throughout her own childhood. In her autobiography, *Blue Remembered Hills*, she writes of her illness:

> [D]isabled children often have an odd unawareness of how it is with them. They know they cannot do certain things which other children can do. They know, as it were, in theory, but they have not yet got the full impact. Soon, all too soon, they become aware of subtle social barriers, the full implication and likely effect on their lives, the loneliness.

Mother's diaries describe just such a moment. Her illness had kept her away from school for several months and, when she returned, she was told she must repeat the previous year. She was outraged.

Previously, she had been among the top of her class, with an established group of friends but now found herself demoted to the same grade as her younger sister. In her diary, sometime around the age of twelve, she reflected:

> It was hard. Some of my old friends snub me, others are sorry for me. The grade six girls treat me as a senior, not as a friend. If I had not had my sister in the same grade, I would have cried.

My aunt, Merridy, remembers the era well, largely because she bore the brunt of Mother's frustration. She was surprised to see herself listed as a source of consolation.

As children the two of them shared a small bedroom. Mother cordoned off part of it for a botanical laboratory, housing her collection of mosses, small plants, and an aquarium full of flat worms. Even at that age she was immensely messy. Her various biological experiments combined with her discarded clothes, books, papers, and used plates until the room became unliveable.

When my aunt objected, Mother dismissed her as if she was delivering some sort of life lesson. Decades later, she would still boast about it, chuckling, 'Merridy thought the world needed to be orderly. But that's not how the world works!' When my aunt recalls the event, fifty years after the fact, she becomes paralysed with frustration.

As Mother's health slowly returned, her personality became progressively more forceful and these sorts of conflicts became increasingly common. In her diary, she reflected:

> I am proud of my illness for I have a reason to grow healthy. To show people I am not a piece of glass that is very delicate.

At school, she baited her teachers with indecipherable handwriting and uneven margins, out of which emerged answers that were inevitably correct. When she did get something wrong, she argued the point until they began to doubt themselves.

She reserved the worst of her behaviour for my grandmother. Of all of my relatives they were the most alike, with a relationship intensified by the traumas of Mother's illness. Their primary point of difference was that Gran, unlike my mother, was innately tidy. It was upon this point Mother aimed her attacks.

From the beachhead of her botanic laboratory, she sprayed mess out across the house. Inevitably, my grandmother objected and the two of them began a circular argument that lasted for the rest of their lives. I observed numerous episodes of it, but never really understood it. During times of stress, Gran would lecture Mother on housekeeping, and Mother would roundly rebuke her. On rare occasions, Gran would launch a sortie to our house while we were out, savagely cleaning the kitchen, bathroom, and living room. When we returned home, Mother would become apocalyptic.

'It's my house!' she would roar, 'I'm a grown woman! She needs to learn to mind her own business!'

Then she would phone my grandmother and they would embark on one of their arguments. It took me years to recognise these incidents were never really about tidiness, and certainly had little to do with housekeeping.

It was not until after Mother died, and I read through her diaries, I began to identify their pattern. There was, of course, no cure for her illness. Naturally, this caused a great deal of fear. My grandmother feared she couldn't protect my mother from death, and my mother feared the grief her death would cause. Their debates about housekeeping reduced that fear into a relatively comprehensible discussion as to how one imposed order on one's daily life.

I witnessed first-hand the supreme energy of these arguments. It would be wrong to say they played no role in my mother's survival. They were like two poker players, defined by their opposing positions but embroiled in the same game. As they argued, they passed their cards back and forth, shaping and reshaping the world around them.

4

> Wilfulness becomes a connecting tissue between a mother and daughters. — Sara Ahmed

Had they been born two or three centuries earlier, I think my mother and grandmother would both have been burnt as witches. As it was, I often feel they suffered the constraint of living in a time hostile to intelligent women. In response, both cultivated a certain staunchness of character. In Mother's case, this was quite transparent. Even before I read her old diaries, I understood who she was, and how she had come to be that way.

My grandmother's youth is far more opaque. I once pressed her on the family history and she told me it all began one Sunday when she was twelve and sat behind my grandfather in church. He was a year older and had a boil on the back of his neck. My grandmother found it enchanting. It was from this boil our family emerged, like Athena from the head of Zeus. Before this, there was nothing.

It was only when my grandfather entered senility that I learned anything more tangible. Like my mother, Grandpa had a penchant for long stories and, as his cognition declined, they grew more personal. In his final years, he began to speak almost compulsively about his boyhood. It had been, I discovered, quite unpleasant.

Most of his stories began with some detail of industrial

history, and then segued unexpectedly into his boyhood. He had a particular story about visiting a sailing ship which I heard numerous times. It lasted anywhere from thirty minutes to two hours, most of which focused on maritime architecture, the Age of Sail, or the history of colonial trade between Australia and Great Britain. He would follow these themes via his own circuitous routes until, suddenly and unexpectedly, altering his tone.

'When I was a boy my father took me to see one of the last big wind jammers taking on wool. I was, I think, about seven.'

He would then revert back into a discussion of sail construction, or deep-water ports along the South Australian coast. It might be another half hour before his tone would change again.

'At that time, we were living in Clinton, which is a good sixty miles, or about a hundred kilometres, outside of Adelaide. But we went over to Ardrossan to see this windjammer come in from London. There weren't many big sailing ships left by then, so it was quite an event.'

Before his dementia kicked in, the story would reach this point and then disappear into an analysis of the difference between a barque and a barquentine. In senility, however, it remained in the realm of the personal. 'I remember holding my father's hand and the two of us looking up into the rigging. After that, my mother died, and we moved down to the city.'

His mother had died giving birth to his sister, who died a few hours later. They moved to the city because the Great Depression had begun, and there was no work in the country. Afterwards, his father joined an offshoot Methodist church, devoid of formal clergy and driven by fire-and-brimstone lay preachers. Some years later it was formally listed as a cult. My grandmother and her parents were members of the congregation.

Gran's father was an enthusiastic member of the congregation, regularly adding his own monologues to the weekly sermons, and pointedly explaining to her that wilful women were the work of the devil.

'He was a shit,' she told me.

'And you didn't like the religion?'

'No. It was boring. As far as I could tell, the purpose of religion was to give boring old men a captive audience for their boring old sermons.'

So it was that she came to sit behind my grandfather, transfixed by his boil. For several weeks, she watched him picking at it while the preachers droned on. When they finally spoke, she was delighted to discover he also found the sermons dull. The two of them began to spend their Sunday afternoons together.

Sometime in the summer of 1944, when they were aged fifteen and sixteen respectively, and the rest of the world was distracted by the war, they thought they invented sex. This was one of the few facets of family history my grandmother regularly divulges of her own volition.

'Our church banned pretty much everything you might want to do as a young person. Sex was the only thing they hadn't expressly prohibited,' she told me, 'so it was sort of inevitable.'

By the armistice, she was pregnant with their first child, although they were still underage. The church elders raised the threat of forcible adoption on the grounds they were unable to provide a stable home. In response, they married and, with loans from their extended family, obtained a cheap block of heavily forested land in the hills, cleared it, and carved their house into the underlying bedrock. They had no mechanical help but smashed through the shale and granite with pick axes and force of will, abandoning their faith in God as they progressed. It was here they raised their four children.

The early days of the family were described with a definite Old Testament character. Shortly after they built the house, a raging fire stormed through the forest around them, came to the back fence, and retreated beneath my grandmother's withering glare. After that, snakes infested the yard. When one of them made its way indoors, my grandmother chased it with a broom, and it disappeared behind the stove and died. They could not extract it and, for several weeks, the house stank of decaying snake.

Later, an earthquake left a large a crack running through the side of the house, which my grandfather patched up with concrete. As a child, this was shown to me as proof of both my grandfather's ingenuity and the resilient foundations of the family itself.

Their experience was not entirely unique. The population of Australia doubled after the Second World War, buoyed partly by the baby boom and partly by the influx of two million migrants from the bombed-out cities of Europe. To house them all, huge swathes of forest and farmland were hastily re-zoned, creating the vast suburbs now characteristic of the Australian city.

By 1960, so many Australians were living in the suburbs that the architect Robyn Boyd called them 'Australia's main contribution to civilization', concluding:

> The suburb is Australia's greatest achievement (not 'proudest' achievement; there is little or no collective

> pride in the suburb, only a huge collection of individual prides.) More people, per head of population, over a longer time, have enjoyed here the dear millstone of a detached house, separated from the next by at least eight feet, a private den for the family not visited by squire or servant.

Before the advent of building companies set up for the express purpose of suburban construction, many of those houses were built by their intended occupants, most of whom had little or no building experience.

The pace of growth was so rapid there was no time to lay down sewerage or potable water systems. As a result, the percentage of unplumbed houses in Australia steadily increased through the sixties. Gough Whitlam, then Leader of the Opposition, called it 'the most effluent nation in the world.' My grandfather installed a cesspit, built at the bottom of the garden, as well as a number of rain water tanks. However, the haphazard supply of drinking water was probably the trigger for Mother's kidney failure. The house sat at the very edge of the Adelaide metropolitan area, where land was cheapest, and it took more than a decade for the sewerage mains to reach them.

Even now the house remains isolated. The area has since been declared a fire risk, with limitations on increased density. When my mother and her siblings were children it was still mostly gum trees. From the top of their street, one could look down upon the glittering lights of the city, and out over the ocean. They could see the rest of the world, but it was always at a distance.

Behind the house ran a gully, and in the gully ran a creek,

where Mother and her siblings spent most of their time. These were the days before it was assumed any unguarded child would be either crushed by a car or kidnapped, and they roamed as they pleased.

Mother's first encounters with the outside world were mostly medical. Her kidneys started to fail sometime around her second birthday. Every week, Gran drove her down to the hospital in the city to see the doctors. For both of them, it was a formative and deeply unpleasant experience.

One night, Mother was left alone in hospital. She had not known this would happen and blamed my grandmother. After she died, I found an entry in one of her diaries, written sometime in her mid-twenties. One of her earliest memories, she wrote, was of being placed in the hospital cot:

> I remember watching my mother leave, she talking to other children, me standing crying, eventually sitting, banging my head on the bars, curling up with my eyes open.

She came to a conclusion most of us don't reach until we're much older: that her mother could not protect her. She can't have been more than three at the time, but held on to the sentiment.

When she was twelve, and recovering from her surgery, she wrote out a quote, attributed to Anne Frank's father, 'All children must look after their own upbringing. Parents can only help.' My grandmother took the polar opposite position. She became aggressively maternal, developing a reputation for belittling doctors and striking fear in the hearts of the nursing staff.

After the surgery, Mother grew slowly stronger. By the age of thirteen, she had recovered enough that her doctors tentatively suggested she might be cured. By sixteen she had begun to fill her diaries with her hopes for the years ahead:

> I was wondering why everyone (including me) at one time or the other longs for adventure. Then what is adventure? I think adventure is merely doing something different. It used to be an adventure to go to the shopping centre but now we go that way every day for five days a week. Once you have had one small adventure you look for a bigger one.

By seventeen, she had exhausted the adventures available from the confines of her parents' house and was eager to make her way out into the world. It was not an attitude my grandmother supported.

At eighteen, Mother finished high school and was offered a position at Teachers College. My grandparents were delighted. At one of the first tutorials, Mother's tutor pulled her aside and explained he was very pleased to see her in his class. When she asked why, he told her girls from the working classes had not previously gone to college. He seemed quite enthused at the prospect and wished her well. Mother was surprised. She had, I think, a vague sense that her family were working class, but only in the sense that her father worked in a factory. As she described it to me, her college years were a time of profound revelations, and the dawning of her independence.

She abandoned her diary when she finished high school and did not begin writing again until she had almost finished her diploma, resuming with the simple addendum, 'Engaged (?) to be married' followed by 'Have become a radical.'

When she announced her engagement, Gran told her she was making a mistake. 'He'll never look after you as well as I can,' she warned.

Mother took this as the height of maternal patronage and flew into a righteous fury. 'I don't care what you think. It's my life, and I'm getting married!'

The resulting conflict became the stuff of family folklore. All subsequent fights between the two of them were measured against it. Only one other argument reached the same heated pinnacle. This occurred two weeks before Mother died. By then, she was confined to the renal ward while her doctors trialled various last-ditch solutions to extend her life. By coincidence, my grandmother was also in hospital, having fainted and banged her head.

Fortunately, they were in different hospitals, on opposite sides of the city. They had been arguing for weeks. At some point, one of them phoned the other and they launched their last, and most furious, debate. It was so heated it could be heard across their respective wards.

Afterwards, Mother had a visit from the head nurse. 'You shouldn't speak to your mum like that,' she said.

Mother called me and admitted she felt somewhat ashamed. 'The problem with your grandmother is she doesn't think I can take care of myself. I'm a grown woman!'

'I don't think she's trying to insult you,' I said, 'I just think she's very worried.'

She paused briefly, but it was hard to tell if she was listening. 'Your grandmother never entirely forgave me for growing up and leaving home. Even now, after all these years, she keeps telling me I should move back in with her and your grandfather. She still thinks she can protect me.'

The problem, she insisted, was that my grandmother held an unnecessarily negative worldview, which made her unable to distinguish inevitable change from impending disaster. I had heard this argument before, although it seemed incongruous given the circumstances.

'It was just like this when I left home,' she continued, 'We had a colossal fight. She told me no one could look after me as well as she could. It was outrageous.'

'That was almost fifty years ago,' I suggested, 'maybe you should just apologise to her?'

To the best of my knowledge she did not. Indeed, I never did figure out exactly what they were arguing about. Two weeks later, Mother began the final descent that led to her death, and the subject was put to rest.

At Mother's funeral, my grandmother arrived late and furious. She sat with my aunt in the back row, shivering with rage. After the burial, she calmed down.

'Why were you so angry?' my aunt asked her.

'I was angry at her for dying,' she admitted.

At the wake, Gran found herself at the centre of a small crowd of Mother's friends. They were all lesbians of a similar age, and afforded her the respect they gave to an unmistakable matriarch. They had, it turned out, heard a great deal about her. Gran seemed quite flattered.

'What was Dimity like as a child?' they asked. 'She wasn't that different. Pretty bossy.' 'When did you know she was gay?'

'It was after she left home. And after she got married.' 'What did you think when she got married?'

Gran thought back to the day my mother had married my father. I had seen pictures of it: the two of them at the registry office, and then posing for photographs outside my grandparents' house. My father grinning nervously, my mother frowning.

'Those two were as gay as each other.' Certainly, the marriage did not prove successful.

5

> The role of housewife, behind whose isolation is hidden social labour, must be destroyed.
> — Mariarosa Dalla Costa and Selma James

Mother's foray into heterosexuality was brief but not without its joys. She met my father at college, where he was studying librarianship. He was two years younger than her, aged just nineteen, and obsessed with folk music, film, and the comedy of Monty Python.

She thought he had a delightfully boyish charm. 'He was very good at being silly, which was a quality I hadn't really encountered before,' she told me. 'And he made me feel mature.'

When they got engaged, both of their mothers thought they were too young. They pointed this out with varying degrees of tact. 'His mum said she'd buy him a new record player if he called off the wedding. I thought he was being very adult when he turned it down.'

'What did Gran think?'

'Well, we stopped talking about it after a while.' I never understood why she had married at all.

'It was the done thing,' she said, 'You got a job, you got married, and then you were an adult.'

She must have had some doubt. After announcing the engagement, she declared they would embark on a 'trial cohabitation', renting a house together in one of the new suburbs on the other side of town. If it went badly, she told my grandmother, she would re-consider the situation.

Her first encounter with feminism happened around the same time. She had taken up a part-time job babysitting for a woman who subscribed to the Women's Electoral Lobby newsletter. It was, at the time, the foremost mouthpiece of feminist politics in Australia and its editors were under surveillance by ASIO. In one of her later diaries, Mother remembered:

> I became involved in the Women's Liberation movement by reading the WEL newsletters of a woman for whom I babysat. I was also caring for the father's children, they being one and the same, but since she did all the organising and paying I thought of them as her children and their faults as her fault. This was in 1972. Her books, conversation, and the newsletter made me feel grumpy and dissatisfied.

Still, she made her way through the back issues, signed up to the local chapter of Women's Lib, and joined a reading group where she read Adrienne Rich's poems and Sheila Rowbotham's histories.

Just before her 'trial' with my father, Mother read Pat Mainardi's iconic essay 'The Politics of Housework.' She was impressed by its analysis of the division of household labour between men and women:

> We both had careers, both had to work a couple of days a week to earn enough to live on, so why shouldn't we share the housework? So I suggested it to my mate and he agreed-most men are too hip to turn you down flat.

> You're right, he said. It's only fair. Then an interesting thing happened. I can only explain it by stating that we women have been brainwashed more than even we can imagine. Probably too many years of seeing television women in ecstasy over their shiny waxed floors or breaking down over their dirty shirt collars. Men have no such conditioning. They recognize the essential fact of housework right from the very beginning. Which is that it stinks.

Mother discussed it with my father and, true to Mainardi's prediction, he did not turn her down, happily agreeing to an equal division of labour within the home.

In practice, neither of them did any housework and the house fell into disarray. Dishes piled up in the kitchen, and unwashed laundry spread across the floor. My father's cat viewed his drum kit as a toilet. Twice a day, my parents would hear the sound of him climbing into the kick drum, and then a low percussive thrum as he sprayed urine against the drum skin. Mother rescued two terrier puppies from the local pound, which she named Suzie (after Suzie Quatro) and Cassie (after Mama Cass). They spent their days yapping furiously and digging up the back yard.

After their first rent inspection, my parents were evicted on the grounds of poor housekeeping and unruly pets. Mother argued it was because the landlord was a staunch Catholic who objected to renting a house to an unmarried couple. Undeterred, Mother declared the 'trial cohabitation' a success and married my father at the Registry Office on the auspicious day of Friday, October the thirteenth, 1972.

By then she had graduated, and taken up her first permanent teaching placement at a school in an impoverished neighbourhood in the inner western suburbs. Her diary documents a discussion with a small boy who explained his family had taken to housebreaking because they were devoid of both cash and marketable skills. He wanted to discuss the moral implications of their crimes.

She raised this with her colleagues but they had little interest in the boy's conundrum. Instead, she was given photocopied pictures, instructed to have her class colour them in, and allocate grades based on the neatness of their work. She thought it unfair:

> The majority of children in my school are in poverty. They do not receive any extra attention or educational advantage at the school. In fact, they suffer due to a lack of understanding of their oppressions.

She considered her own education, when she had been held back after her childhood illness, and made to feel dim-witted. She decided her fellow teachers were on the wrong side of history. It was an attitude that remained with her for the following four decades, and fuelled both her career and an almost constant series of conflicts with her more conservative colleagues.

While her politics grew increasingly radical, she entered her only sustained period of a socially conventional lifestyle. My parents took out a mortgage on a small house in the suburb of Plympton, previously owned by the State Housing Commission. Mother purchased a new Datsun 180b and took an interest in fashion. My father collected records and joined a folk band. On weekends, the two of them attended dinner parties, where his friends would belittle her interest in feminism, and he would blush as she yelled at them.

When they reached their first wedding anniversary, Mother reflected, 'Seem to get on well. Have learnt not to take all my feminist anger out on him.' The two of them had attained all the trappings of adulthood: they were married, with good jobs and their own house. She could not understand why she felt so discontented.

I sometimes wonder what my father made of the situation. By that point, he was almost certainly having affairs outside the marriage, with both men and women. I assume he wasn't happy but I never knew him well enough to ask. After they divorced, he remarried and quickly resumed living in much the same manner. 'I think he enjoyed the security,' Mother used to tell me, 'but it made me feel trapped.'

Around the time of their second wedding anniversary, Mother sat down with her diary and took stock of her situation. Her life was, she admitted, materially very comfortable, and yet immensely unfulfilling. She concluded:

> In 1974, I went to work (teaching), left home, and moved in with my lover. Five months later, I married the same lover, and quite consciously changed my surname. Now I walk around groaning, 'What have I done?'

She started spending more time at Women's Lib meetings and joined various sub-committees and consciousness raising groups.

She also began to spend more time with my grandmother. Gran joined her at various lectures, marches, and rallies. At one point, they both attended a pro-choice rally, quite a radical outing for a mother and daughter in the early 1970s. Mother wrote a lengthy diary entry about it, nearly all of which focuses on an argument they had about one of the acts performing at the rally: an all-lesbian jug band called 'The Shameless Hussies'. My grandmother thought they were terrible, Mother thought they were wonderful, and they had a heated discussion on the topic.

Feminism was in its second wave, and they both found it exciting. Writing about it a few years later Mother remembered, 'It was the beginning of making changes in my life, of actually choosing a direction.' I think Gran appreciated it for the same reason. In contrast to the staunch Methodism of her own youth, it offered the promise of choice.

At some point in 1975, the two of them attended a workshop on feminist pedagogy, where Mother was asked for her opinions on gender equality among primary school students. She wrote about it in her diary with such enthusiasm the entry is almost illegible. Across several scrawled pages, only one passage can be deciphered:

> You can't teach an idea so that it becomes a way of thinking. You present it [illegible] the mind to [illegible] it and leave it to be absorbed and acted upon. Ideas of behaviour I mean. Such as sexual equality.

After the workshop, she returned home to find my father had consumed several bags of potato chips, a box of chocolates, and a large bottle of soda. Afterwards, he became so nauseated he threw up.

By the time of their third anniversary, my parents had already begun to drift apart. As a side effect of her interest in feminism, Mother had met, and befriended, lesbians for the first time. Of these early encounters she wrote, 'I wish I could find out what it is like to be with a woman. I know I would have no difficulty loving a woman.' That she did not act on this sooner probably owes more to the rapidly declining state of her health than any improvement in her marriage.

Three years into the marriage, Mother's kidney function collapsed entirely, and she became even sicker than she had been as a child. As she grew weaker, her tolerance for my father dissolved. 'It wasn't that he did anything particularly wrong,' she once told me. 'But he just wanted to be an ordinary, middle-class man, and I couldn't think of anything duller. I suppose we might have stayed together. It was a very comfortable and easy life. But I didn't think I had that much longer to live, so I suppose I wasn't thinking about comfort.'

6

> The figs fall from the trees, they are good and sweet; and in falling the red skins of them break. A north wind I am to ripe figs… Imbibe now their juice and their sweet substance! It is autumn all around, and clear sky, and afternoon. — Frederick Nietzsche

By the time of my parents' fourth wedding anniversary, Mother's doctors had begun to worry. Her childhood surgery had only delayed her kidney problem. She underwent a series of examinations, after which they concluded one of her kidneys had died, and the other was barely functioning. She would not, they thought, live far into her thirties, nor could she expect much of her remaining years.

Mother described her illness as being like a fog: she could neither think nor feel clearly. Her failing kidneys left her blood full of toxins, dulling her senses and making it hard to concentrate. All food took on an unpleasant metallic taste, and she became so thin she could see the outline of the bones in her legs and arms. Paradoxically, as her weight dropped she began to feel heavier, as if the force of gravity had increased exponentially.

My father tried to console her but wasn't very good at it. She found his repetitive performance of Monty Python skits tiring. Nor was he much help in any practical sense. One cold winter night, a storm broke out, torrential rain fell upon their house, and the gutters overflowed. Mother insisted my father go outside, fetch the ladder from the shed, and unblock the drainpipes. He refused and continued to watch television. In a rage, she wrapped herself in her duffle coat, stormed outside and ascended to the roof, returning soaked and covered in leaf mulch. He looked shamefaced but did not shift from his place in front of the television.

Gran began to worry. Each week, when she knew Mother was at work, she drove down from the hills and cleaned my parents' house. Mother hadn't asked her to and, when she returned to find the house clean, she took it as an insult. Her diary of the time includes something that's either a poem or an edict, addressed to my grandmother:

> The care and cleanliness of this house is the responsibility
> of the two people who live here.
>
> The discomfort which may be caused by their methods
> of 'housekeeping' is their discomfort.
>
> Remember I am not a housewife because I never
> married a house.

The two of them stopped attending Women's Lib events together. They both grew terse and angry.

One morning, too ill to go to work, Mother sat in the shower and cried. She was, she admitted, sad, although it was not the illness itself that bothered her. Her friends and colleagues now treated her as frail. She found their sympathy patronising. She was placed on indefinite sick leave.

'Being very sick,' she once explained, 'is very hard work. But people think you're like a Dickens character, laying about doing nothing, waiting to die.'

'You mean like Little Nell?' I asked.

'I hate Little Nell. Dickens was stupid.'

Mother's doctors put her on dialysis. She was obliged to spend several mornings each week in hospital, plugged into a machine that drained the blood from her body, cleaned it, and then pumped it back in via a vein in her arm.

Gran used this time to stage increasingly frequent and aggressive cleaning raids. When Mother returned from hospital, she would find her house sparkling. This led to a spectacular conflict, ostensibly caused by an otherwise innocuous magazine rack.

The magazine rack itself was worthless. Mother had pulled it out of hard rubbish, that suburban ritual where people leave their unwanted furniture by the side of the road, for collection by either the local council or their thrifty neighbours. She thought it was a very respectable addition to her household and gave it pride of place in the living room.

Gran, on other hand, thought it was rubbish. Each week, when she cleaned the house, she dragged it out of the living room and in to the shed. A few hours later, Mother would arrive home, drag it back from the shed into the living room, and then phone my grandmother to complain. The two of them would argue for an hour or so, wait two days, and then begrudgingly forgive each other, only to repeat the routine the following week. This went on for several months until, on the fifteenth of December, 1976, Mother was unexpectedly given a kidney transplant.

'I was twenty-four,' she later wrote, 'and I went in for my

usual dialysis appointment. I noticed the nurses whispering. Half an hour later, they were wheeling me in for the operation.'

The previous evening a heavy rain had descended upon the suburbs of Adelaide and a young man, out riding his motorcycle, lost control and crashed with fatal consequences. Fortunately, he had bequeathed his organs to posterity. At eleven o'clock the following morning, one of his kidneys was transplanted into my mother. She woke up in the early afternoon feeling surprisingly well.

In those days, organ transplants had a success rate of around one in four, with most failing in the first two months. Mother shared the renal ward with a young man named Malcolm, and a woman in her late thirties called Mrs Ellbourne. Malcolm contracted pneumonia, his transplant failed, and he died after less than a week. A fortnight later, Mrs Ellbourne's body rejected the transplanted organ. My mother could hear her weeping from pain through the night, growing slowly quieter until she died the following morning.

A month later, when Mother was released from hospital, my grandmother took her to the Botanic Gardens. It was early autumn, and they walked along in silence, surveying the changing colour of the leaves.

'I've been very ill, haven't I?' my mother asked. Gran agreed she had been very ill indeed.

'But I'm not ill now!' she announced, kicking her way through a pile of fallen leaves.

Three months later, when she was still alive, Mother wrote, 'I didn't know the risks, thank goodness.' After six months, with her health continuing to improve, her doctors declared the operation a success. They tentatively estimated she would live for at least another decade.

The ill-fated magazine rack was forgotten, although the arguments about it became part of family folklore. Following any disagreement with Gran, Mother would recount them in the tone of Aesop's fables.

'Once, I had a magazine rack. I got it out of hard rubbish. It was very good, so I put it in the living room. But then your grandmother snuck into the house while I was out, and dragged it into the shed.'

I heard the story thousands of times, but never understood the exact point she was making, nor learned what actually happened to the magazine rack. The moral, however, was quite clear. It operated much like something out of Frederich Nietzsche's *Thus Spoke Zarathustra*:

> And you yourselves should create what you have hitherto called the world: the world should be formed in your image by your reason, your will and your love!

There was the world, and then there was Mother, and her mother. Within the world, there were any number of objects, be they magazine racks or broken kidneys, upon which the two of them exercised their will, creating a new and better world in the process.

Over the course of that autumn, Mother grew progressively stronger. As she did so, she grew ever less satisfied with the state of her life. She resumed her participation in Women's Lib, attending talks, lectures, and reading groups, and began studying Simone de Beauvoir's *The Second Sex*.

Why, she asked herself, had she married? She had thought it

was just what you did; a necessary precursor to the independence of adulthood. In her diary, she wrote:

> Marriage provides a cop out to taking control of your life, yourself, your humanity. To be given a chance at life – I don't want to waste it on housework and a burdensome husband.

The house grew ever messier, and my father found his place increasingly uncertain.

Still, the marriage had not become loveless. In the months leading up to her sixth wedding anniversary, her diary contains a one line entry: 'I'm pregnant.' My grandmother was furious. The doctors had made it quite clear pregnancy produced dire risks for kidney transplant recipients but Mother wanted a child and decided to ignore them.

After four months 'lying up' to prevent a miscarriage, an ultrasound found the foetus had died. This, her doctors reminded her, was what they had expected. She had been prescribed corticoids to keep her transplanted kidney alive, and these, they explained, had probably stopped the foetus from developing.

She writes little about it in her diary. When I was growing up, we only discussed her miscarriage once. When I was four I had a rather intense dream of having an older sister.

'Well,' she explained, 'you sort of do, except she was never born.'

Her doctors had told her the child would have been a girl. She never told me whether she had chosen a name, or how she felt about it.

I know the miscarriage must have affected her. It occurred, according to her diary, on October twenty-fifth, 1978, just as the jacarandas were coming into bloom. In November, she went on a camping trip with a group of her friends from Women's Lib. It was here she met June. They shared a tent for two nights. In her diary, she wrote, 'One night we made love, and one we didn't.' It was the beginning of the next phase of her life.

7

> The earth trembles before our collision as we walk a path this side of loneliness, and that side of what can be known through words alone – that side of revolution and madness – and everywhere love.
> — From 'In Amerika They Call Us Dykes', in *Our Bodies, Ourselves*

After her first encounter with June, Mother told my father she was having an affair. He admitted to his own dalliances with both men and women. They had a frank yet civil discussion on the state of things and declared theirs would be an open marriage. Mother arranged a lunch so he could meet June. For a few months, things settled down.

It has become common to present the 1960s and 70s as a time of sexual liberation, in which such open marriages were normal, and the grim conventions of the fifties were at an end. This is something of a myth. Writing in 1973, Sheila Rowbotham, reflected, 'Much of the talk of permissive society and sexual liberation means merely permission to consume.' In her description, it was a great time for pornographers and wife-swapping parties, but these are not inherently liberating.

I have my mother's copy of Rowbotham's *Women's Consciousness, Man's World*, with her married name written in biro on the inside cover alongside the date: 1977, the same year she met June. Based on Mother's descriptions, I got the impression my parents' infidelity lessened the yoke of marriage, but did not make either of them feel particularly free.

'We stayed married for the same reason we got married in the first place,' she told me, 'I didn't know there was an alternative.'

Adrienne Rich later described it as an era of 'compulsory heterosexuality'. Whatever the spectacle of 'free love', Rich wrote:

> [T]he absence of choice remains the great unacknowledged reality, and in the absence of choice, women will remain dependent on the chance or luck of particular relationships and will have no collective power to determine the meaning and place of sexuality in their lives.

Is sexuality a choice? Most people, myself included, would say no. On the other hand, many people of my parents' age chose to repress their sexuality, out of fear, or insecurity, or a simple desire to fit in.

When my mother married, homosexuality was still illegal, treated alternately as a vice or a mental health problem. It was a risk for someone to acknowledge it, even to themselves. Indeed, a few months before my parents' wedding, a gay man had been attacked and killed at a local beat. The assailants were police officers, who made a regular practice of beating up homosexuals.

In this case, the man happened to be a respected Cambridge educated academic. When the officers were released without charge, the resulting public outcry led to the decriminalization of homosexuality in South Australia, the first state in the nation to do so. Yet even after it was legalised, attitudes remained openly hostile. For several months, local Christian extremists staged a protest, predicting God would unleash a mighty tidal wave, destroying the entire state. The expected disaster never happened but homosexuality remained illegal across much of Australia for a further twenty years.

It has since become common to view this level of bigotry as akin to the archaic rituals of more barbaric times, not unlike witch hunts or the burning of heretics. Yet the policing of sexuality has a long and robust history, frequently concealing itself within seemingly rational public health debates. This quasi-rationality has made it remarkably resilient.

The historian Graham Robb ascribes this resilience to a shift in the mid-nineteenth century, away from describing homosexuality as a sin, and towards treating it as a medical problem. In its early phases, the transition often appears as much farce as tragedy. For example, Robb lists a collection of doctors who ardently believed homosexual men could be identified by their funnel shaped anuses:

> At a medical conference in Berlin in 1890, Carl Liman described a case in which the patient had been probed, in a single session, by eight 'lubricated fingers.' The eight doctors subsequently issued eight reports which all contradicted one another.

This method of diagnosis remained in vogue for some years, until it was discovered that any anus becomes funnel shaped when probed with enough rigor.

Over time, approaches became subtler, but no more logical. In 1913, the German doctor Magnus Hirshfeld declared homosexual men could be detected by their inability to whistle. By contrast, he wrote, lesbians whistled compulsively.

He claimed to know a pair who toured the music halls, performing a professional whistling act. From there, the treatment of homosexuality was absorbed into the field of psychoanalysis, where it spent much of the twentieth century being blamed on childhood trauma, bad mothering, and a litany of other causes.

By the sixties, it was being treated with 'ice pick' lobotomies and electroshock therapy. Case notes on one such program, conducted by American psychologist Robert Heath in the early seventies, noted that, after treatment, patients usually 'developed a generalized terror.' The documentary *Witches, Faggots, Dykes and Poofters*, made in Sydney in 1980 (the same year I was born) features a woman younger than my mother who had been lobotomised.

When I was a child, it was still common for homosexuality to be described as somewhere between a sin and a sickness. When the AIDS virus first appeared in the early eighties, it was labelled Gay-Related Immune Deficiency. In 1983, the American politician Pat Buchanan said of it:

> The sexual revolution has begun to devour its children. And among the revolutionary vanguard, as Gay rights activists, the mortality rate is highest and climbing… the poor homosexuals – they have declared war upon nature, and now nature is exacting an awful retribution.

I remember hearing these sorts of comments when I was a child. When Mother, and most of her friends, came out, such attitudes were unavoidable. It took a considerable force of character to reject them.

In this respect, my mother had one particular advantage. She had spent a good part of her life listening to medical professionals tell her she was too weak to live and, as such, had a healthy scepticism toward their opinions. As a result, she was largely immune to the quasi-medical moralism of the times. Her recovery from the transplant, and the realisation of her sexuality, occurred in almost perfect unison.

With her new kidney functioning almost normally, she lost all tolerance for convention. In her diary she wrote, 'I want to be different, I'm complimented when people call me a character.' She enjoyed the material comforts of her married life — the steady income, nice furniture, weekends away and so on — but hated the cloying sense of conformity.

The few photographs I have from the era capture her transformation. She had always been thin, fey, and long-haired. After the transplant, she cut her hair and started wearing dungarees. In most photos, she is blurred as if she couldn't stand still long enough for the photographer to capture her. It was the version of her I knew growing up.

I don't think it was just her sexuality that brought out her sense of difference. On the contrary, I think surviving the transplant brought her into touch with the depth of her own character, unleashing a force of will that washed aside the trappings of heterosexual life. It was, as her writing from the time shows, not an easy process.

For some months, her marriage continued alongside her affair with June. Over time, however, she noted my father had grown uncharacteristically sad. His own affairs were shallow in nature, written off by my mother as boyish hijinks more than active infidelity. Eventually, she forced him into a lengthy conversation about June. At first, he insisted he was entirely supportive, but under duress admitted he was quite upset. When she pressed him on why he hadn't objected earlier, he somewhat pitifully said he wanted her to have a 'nice time.' He had not expected her to fall in love with someone else.

In Mother's estimation, my father enjoyed the stability of married life, despite his sporadic infidelity. Unlike her, he took comfort in the conventional nature of their union and worried about her increasing dissatisfaction. I think he quite sincerely loved her, and remained enthralled by the force of her character even as it worked against him. In the final years of the marriage, he was clearly nervous. In an effort to win her approval, he increased his self-improvement campaign: dieting, exercising, and even undertaking basic household chores.

Mother felt sorry for him, which is a poor foundation for a relationship. At the same time, June's hypochondria had also begun to frustrate her. She had hoped polyamory would make her feel less constrained but instead found herself doubly frustrated. In March of 1979, three years after her kidney transplant, she told both of them she was going on holiday, and that neither of them would be coming with her.

She spent two weeks in a rented shack outside the isolated township of Dutton, reading an anthology called *Our Bodies, Ourselves*, published in the US a few years earlier. It had an entire chapter on, and by, lesbians, beginning:

> This chapter is a beginning, the beginning of our efforts to define for ourselves what it means to be a lesbian in

> this society. It is part of a larger beginning, as more and more gay women throughout the country have stated to write, argue, sing, and shout their message to the straight world.

Otherwise, she wandered through the scrub with her dogs, subsisted on a diet of mince, onions, and tea, and thought about her future. She had bought a new diary for the occasion, reflecting:

> I keep thinking of June saying how we needed a country drive. Perhaps I should have invited her but that would defeat my purpose of being alone.

Dutton is neither the most exciting nor picturesque of towns but as a place to be alone it is unrivalled. Hardly anyone lives there and the closest thing to a tourist attraction is a Lutheran church.

The merits of being alone make up the majority of the numerous diary entries she made there, conspicuously at odds with her decision to simultaneously remain both married and have an affair. On the third day of her stay, she wrote out a short audit of her circumstances:

> Aged twenty-six years and nine months, married almost six years. A habitual heterosexual with strong lesbian tendencies.

She identified three paths stretching out before her. She could remain married, possibly have children, and continue to enjoy the sedate but financially comfortable life of a middle-class heterosexual. She could leave my father, move in with June, and adopt a homosexual version of the same life. The third option was to pursue a life entirely on her own.

It took her less than a week to decide, permanently and irrevocably, upon this final path. She saw it as an affirmation of her own autonomy; proof she had chosen her destiny rather than taken the path of least resistance. The few negatives she identified were mostly material: the loss of her marital home, the security of a double income, and the risk she would never have a child. Of the personal cost — loneliness, isolation, and the lack of love and companionship — she made no mention.

I'm not sure there was much my father or June could have done to change her mind. I suppose anyone who survives a mortal threat will come away from the experience changed, and changed in a way that is difficult to describe, even to those closest to them. In her rented shack in Dutton, Mother tried for the first time to articulate who she had become since her transplant. She conceded that her survival was partly the result of improvements in medical science, but mostly she credited it to herself.

Over the fortnight of her holiday, she concluded that she had been afraid of her sickness and impending death but, having survived, she could not tolerate the compromises and comfortable habits of middle-class life. The realisation of her homosexuality appears to have flowed from this epiphany rather than been the spark for it. Once the decision was reached, she was never in doubt. When she returned from Dutton, she announced she was homosexual, told my father she was leaving him, and began to look for a house of her own.

The very first person she told, even before my father, was her younger sister, Merridy. 'She told me she was a lesbian, and I said, "I know." I think I'd always known, I was just waiting for her to put it into words I suppose.'

'Did you know when you were kids?' I asked her.

'Well, we didn't know what homosexuals were then. But I think before the transplant she was always so sick, it was like she was always a bit watered down. Afterwards, she was operating at full strength and it was a bit frightening to be honest. It was like she went from a light breeze to a powerful storm. I think your father just got blasted out of the way.'

Still, Mother was nervous when she came out to my grandparents. Her friends had given her a series of pamphlets offering counselling services for the parents of homosexuals. My grandmother looked at them briefly and handed them back. 'I don't need counselling to have a gay child,' she said. 'Do you have any pamphlets on how to handle a messy daughter?'

'So you don't mind if I'm a lesbian?' Mother asked. 'And that I'm going to get a divorce?'

'I never thought you should get married in the first place, so this just proves my point.'

It took Mother two months to find a new place to live, during which time she continued to live with my father. It was in this period that I was conceived. Her diary suggests the happy event occurred around her birthday on the twenty-eighth of May. It is the last mention she makes of any intimacy between them.

She moved out on the ninth of June, taking out a lease on a battered maisonette in the inner southern suburbs. My father helped her pack her Datsun, and she drove off with their bedding, the stereo, and her two dogs. Her new house was run-down, but the landlord was relaxed, the neighbours friendly, and there was a small garden with a pepper tree in the backyard. She found out she was pregnant two weeks later.

8

There was never a great man who had not a great mother. — Olive Schreiner

I think my mother viewed her pregnancy as a sort of self-induced immaculate conception; a divine gift for the decision she had made during her pilgrimage to Dutton. When she told her doctors, they were aghast and advised her to terminate the pregnancy. She refused, writing:

> I don't want an abortion. I want a strong, free and independent life with a child. But how?

A week later she told June, a handful of friends, and my aunt, but not my father or my grandmother.

It was several weeks before Gran found out. Anticipating a fight, Mother had instructed my aunt to pass on the news. Several hours later, she reported back, clearly shaken.

'How did it go?' Mother asked her.

It had not gone well. Gran had done a good deal of shouting.

The following day, Mother made the executive decision to halve the medications she took for her transplanted kidney, blaming them for her earlier miscarriage. She did not discuss this with her doctors, but simply announced it to Merridy a few days later. As the news filtered through the family it brought the impending conflict with my grandmother to a head. By that point, it was too late for an abortion, and Gran had little option but to accept my mother's position.

I'm not sure when Mother told my father, or how he felt. In her diary she wrote simply, 'He was upset,' but offered no detail. By the time I read her brief description, there was no chance for clarification as she had been dead for a month, and he for almost thirty years. I had never contemplated the subject before because, like Mother, I had assumed she was solely responsible for my existence.

I know my parents remained in contact during the early phases of the pregnancy, but my father gradually and completely disappears from her diary entries. Mother, I suspect, had other things on her mind. Alongside filing for divorce, moving house, and being pregnant, she somehow found time to start a second affair with a woman called Alice.

Unsurprisingly, June and Alice loathed each other, a sentiment Mother did little to counteract. The affair with Alice ended quite quickly after Mother told her she was 'too middle class.' As for June, Mother began lecturing her on her hypochondria and, as the date of my arrival grew closer, they irreconcilably drifted apart.

Whenever Mother told me about this part of her life, she spoke of it as the age when she became who she was born to be. Her writing from the time is more overt about the uncertainties. Right up until my arrival she lived in fear of another miscarriage. When she reached mid-term, she wrote, 'the difference between a foetus and a living person is fear.'

In the final week before my arrival, she dreamt of being in the birthing room, laying on a stainless-steel table. Nothing was quite joined together, but appeared instead to shift like the parts of a mobile. The rings on the curtain rail around the bed did not touch the fabric of the curtain itself. As they moved, she could see the bricks in the wall shifting, allowing a harsh light to pierce the room.

She went into the hospital at the end of January. Her doctors insisted on an induced birth, hoping it would limit the risks. It did not. Mine was not an easy birth, although Mother always made the entire affair sound comic. 'You half crowned, took one look at the world, and then went back in,' she would chuckle.

She told me this story several hundred times, usually after I'd done something stubborn, pessimistic, or generally recalcitrant. She claimed it proved my personality pre-dated my birth, and couldn't be blamed on her. In medical terms, a retreat into the birth canal is usually indicative of a major emergency, and commonly results in death. The doctors panicked, and I was extracted via emergency caesarean, screaming with surprise and dismay.

The date was Friday, the first of February, 1980. Mother claimed the nurses kept me secreted away for the following three days, but it is more likely she was exhausted and delusional. On the third day, we were reunited. To everyone's surprise, I was entirely healthy. I am mentioned in her diary for the first time the following morning:

> Good morning it's Feb 4th and I have a three-day old son. He has character to my amazement. He talks and cries, waves his hands and likes to be awake and watching things. He is curious, which to me is lovely.

> He even smiles though they tell me it is wind. He is to be named Ianto.

My name was a source of conflict between us for some years. She chose it, I think, because it was alien to the Anglo-Australian tongue and she thought it would instill an inescapable sense of individuality.

In practice, it has meant I've spent my entire life explaining its pronunciation ('Yan-toe'), its origins (it is a Welsh name), and my ancestry (I am not Welsh). My grandmother later admitted it took the family several weeks to figure out how to pronounce it, and they referred to me as 'Little Bear' for the better part of a year, presumably because I was small, rotund, and emitted regular grumbling noises.

When my father came to visit, he suggested I should be called George after a professional wrestler called Gorgeous George.

'I thought it was a stupid name,' Mother told me, 'and I told him so. I think he was a bit offended.'

He was trailing his new girlfriend and Mother was unimpressed. We didn't see him again for two years.

After a further week in observation, Mother and I were both in good health and the doctors conceded we could be discharged. She demanded my aunt buy her roses, and allowed my grandparents to drive her home. However, once Mother was back in her own house, she grew unbearably smug. Both Merridy and Gran remember the occasion well.

'I offered to stay with her, but she was keen to get rid of us,' explained Gran, 'She let me buy her a fan because it was an extremely hot summer, and then told us to go away.'

'I think she figured she'd made a whole new person on her own, and didn't need us for anything,' added my aunt, 'She didn't even thank me for getting the roses.'

For the first few weeks, as Mother's caesarean scar healed, the hot weather made it impossible to go outside. Each morning, she placed me in a bassinet in the living room and spent the day laying on the couch, watching me. I became transfixed with the maroon curtains she had hung to keep out the heat.

After a month, I became so engrossed by them she began to fear I had an intellectual impairment. I would frown at them for hours.

Eventually, she concluded I was simply thinking my own thoughts. By three months, I had settled whatever conundrum I found in the curtains, but continued to frown almost constantly. Mother began to suspect my early propensity for smiling had been gas after all. It was not that I cried more than normal babies, but I always seemed to be brooding.

By the age of six months, she began to suspect I had not inherited her innate optimism. On the contrary, I began pulling a frown uncannily like my grandmother's. Mother clung to any indication of good humour. Our family photo albums contain a series of photos of me captioned 'Learning to laugh' in which I am shown making my first awkward forays into light-heartedness. These were intermittent and ultimately unsuccessful.

Still, she remained optimistic. She was free from the constraints of her suitors, unshackled from convention, and thought herself entirely independent. It was as she wished to be. When the weather began to cool, she took me outside into the backyard, where I lay in my bassinette while she gardened. In her diary, she wrote:

> Today I planted eggplant.
>
> Next to the capsicum
>
> The garden grows homely
>
> As I settle down here alone.
>
> There's geranium, lavender
>
> Sage, thyme and nasturtium.
>
> Slowly I'm building a life of my own.

In most of the photographs of me between the ages of four and twelve months, I am depicted in the garden, stuffing lavender, sage or geraniums into my mouth, usually with the same expression of melancholy contemplation.

9

> The feminist agenda is not about equal rights for women. It is about a socialist, anti-family political movement that encourages women to leave their husbands, kill their children, practice witchcraft, destroy capitalism, and become lesbians. — Pat Robertson

In autumn, Mother decided I was big enough to see the world, so she strapped me into my pram and took me to a protest march. Halfway through, she found herself at the front of the crowd, marching alongside a group of other mothers, all pushing prams. They turned a corner to discover a row of mounted police blocking the road. For several tense minutes, the police looked at the women with prams, and then backed their horses away.

The march continued, ending in a park where the usual speakers made the usual speeches. Mother was not impressed. She thought both the police and the march organisers were idiots. She could hardly hear the speakers, who stood on the back of a flatbed truck, yelling into a megaphone. My pram was hard to push across the grass, through the thick crowd, and she needed to go to the toilet.

'Eventually I found some friends, who offered to take care of you while I went to find the toilets,' she told me, 'When I got back, they had disappeared.

And then when I found them, they didn't have you. I was

terrified. I thought you'd been kidnapped. They were all stoned and couldn't understand why I was so upset.'

'Where was I?'

'I found you sitting on the shoulders of a very beautiful, very large, very gay man, watching the speakers. He'd offered to take care of you while my friends were getting stoned. He put you on his shoulders so I could find you in the crowd, because he thought I might be worried.'

'Was I upset?' I asked.

'No, you were the same as usual. You were frowning.'

She wrote about the incident in her diary, listing it as her first serious encounter with a protective maternal urge:

> No matter where my child is I know
>
> What my mother knew In fact
>
> At times I'm her And her mother And her mother too.

She thought back on her illness, and her transplant, and realised how much fear her own mother must have endured. In her diary she concluded, 'My mother gets an 'A' for bravery.' As far as I can tell, she never said anything like this directly to anyone else, let alone to Gran.

She took great pride in her powers of maternal protection. Even when I was well and truly an adult, she would ring me, announce, 'I'm your mother,' and then launch into a long soliloquy of advice. She had an opinion on most of the things I did, or should be doing, no matter how trivial.

'Now, I'm your mother. And I'm worried you're spending too much on coffee, so I've bought you a plunger.'

'Now. I'm your mother, and I'm worried about your cholesterol. I think you should get your cholesterol checked.'

Three days before her death, as we sat together in the hospice, she told me, 'It isn't fair. You need your mother.' I was almost forty by that point, living in Sydney with Diana, and entirely independent, but I had read that parents often feel guilty when they die so I tried to reassure her.

'I don't need you. I just wish we had another decade or two. But I don't need you, I'll be okay.'

She looked disappointed. In retrospect, I think it was the wrong thing to say. Motherhood had been the affirmation of her strength, freedom, and independence. She didn't want to relinquish the sense of power it gave her, even though she was on the cusp of death.

I sometimes ask myself if other mothers feel this way, or if there was something unique about our relationship. As a child, I would hear my friends talk about their mothers, or watch the families on television, and think she was so unlike them.

In at least one important respect, she was undeniably different. When I was born, it was still shameful to be a single mother, and the idea of a lesbian producing a child — let alone a son — bordered on the unthinkable. IVF was not widely available, homosexuals weren't allowed to adopt, and fathers usually won custody in the divorce courts. I've never met anyone older than me from a family like mine.

Her attitude to motherhood was shaped by that sense of difference, although I find it hard to tell exactly how as I have so few points of comparison. In *Our Bodies, Ourselves* there's an essay on what it was like to be a lesbian and a mother, written a few years before I was born:

> In a society that is afraid of lesbians and wants to shelter its children from 'queers', being a lesbian mother is very hard. Telling friends and relatives about being gay can be hard for anyone, but if you're a mother, they can try to put added guilt on you. They will say, 'What are you going to do with the children? What will their friends think?'

From a very young age, I knew people disapproved of our family, and I knew it was dangerous to talk openly about our life. I don't recall being told I should be careful, but was always aware of the risk. It created an aura of fear, which I don't think is common among heterosexual families.

Mother noticed it around the time of my first birthday. When she took me out in my pram, we were regularly frowned at, or treated curtly. When we did the weekly shopping, she was trailed by the store detective. For most of my childhood, we avoided Salvation Army op shops because she thought they were bigoted.

'When you were almost one,' she explained, 'I was buying some pants and the lady at the counter asked how old you were. I thought she was being nice, so I said you were almost one. And then she looked down at you and asked if you were a mistake. I didn't say anything, so then she asked if I regretted having you.'

'But how did she know you weren't married?'

'Well, I had my Women's Lib badge on, and I was wearing my dungarees.'

'Did she know you were lesbian?' I asked.

'I don't think it mattered. She just knew I was different. I started dressing a bit more conservatively. I found people were nicer if I wore floral shirts.'

If anything, the sense of disapproval grew more pronounced as I grew up. Just before my first birthday, Ronald Reagan came into power and people started talking about 'family values' and 'broken families.' In 1998, the year I came of age, Margaret Thatcher said of people like Mother and I:

> It is far better to put these children in the hands of a very good religious organisation, and the mother as well, so that they will be brought up with family values.

Even after Thatcher and Reagan were gone, their legacy remained. When I was in my thirties, Cory Bernardi, a conservative from my home state of South Australian, announced:

> Given the increasing number of 'non-traditional' families, there is a temptation to equate all family structures as being equal or relative…why then the levels of criminality among boys and promiscuity among girls who are brought up in single-parent families, more often than not headed by a single mother?

From the comfort of my middle age, it is easy to laugh off these sorts of comments, but as a boy I found them very frightening. When I was six or seven, I saw the Reverend Fred Nile espousing similar opinions on television and developed a phobia he would turn up on the doorstop and steal me away. I wasn't entirely unjustified. Had I been born a decade or two earlier, I probably would have been put into foster care.

To her dismay, Mother found a sort of inverse bigotry among her own peers. She had expected her feminist friends would be wholly supportive when she had a child, but found their responses mixed. Some felt motherhood was a sign of irrecoverable conformity, others were openly angry although she could not tell why, and many were simply unsure of how to respond.

Just before my first birthday, she took me to one of the various camping trips organised by the local chapter of Women's Lib. There were no facilities for children, and no concessions were made to the pressures of motherhood. In her diary, she wrote:

> Exhausted after lack of support at a Women's Camp, I complained that the camp had a policy for drugs, men, and dogs, but nothing for mothers. I was told that as I had chosen to be a mother it was my problem and the women involved did not feel politically obliged to support me.

She had hoped her comrades would rally to her side, and she might raise me in a feminist utopia. It was a profound disappointment.

I'm told there are now parenting groups for queer families, and children's books with titles like *My Two Mothers and Me*, but in the early eighties I think the rhetoric of 'family values' had become so overwhelming that merely having a family was seen as a commitment to convention.

In fairness, I can understand her friends' reluctance. In the early 1980s, motherhood still usually meant leaving one's job, living off one's husband, and being consigned to the home. There might not have been a strict correlation between motherhood and conformism, but it was extremely difficult to be a mother and a revolutionary. The fear hasn't lessened with time. In 2001, Rachael Cusk wrote of her second pregnancy:

> Motherhood, for me, was a sort of compound fenced off from the rest of the world. I was forever plotting my escape from it, and when I found myself pregnant again when Albertine was six months old I greeted my old cell with the cheerless acceptance of a convict intercepted at large.

Almost twenty years later, and writing about the decision not to have a child, Sheila Heti described a sense of obligation; a pressure to not just become a mother, but to do so at the expense of any other way of living:

> A woman must have children because she must be occupied. When I think of all the people who want to forbid abortions, it seems it can only mean one thing – not that they want this new person in the world, but that they want that woman to be doing the work of child rearing more than they want her to be doing anything else.

In this respect, my mother was very different because nobody wanted her to become a mother. Becoming one made her irrevocably non-conventional. After she got over her initial anger, motherhood made her feel like a revolutionary.

At the same time, I don't think she was immune to the pressures described by other mothers, and nor, in my own way, was I. When I first started telling people about my family, the most common response was a polite bewilderment.

'But how did she have you?' my friends would ask.

I would explain I had been conceived in the normal way and they would stare at me in surprise. I was in my mid-twenties, working on my doctorate, and bore no resemblance to the brow-beaten delinquents they had come to expect from broken homes.

'But how?' they would repeat.

Their questions weren't malicious. Like me, they were struggling with the same myth of what a family should look like, albeit from opposite positions.

Whether we agreed with Reagan and Thatcher or not, it was this spectre we held ourselves up to.

Of course, there were moments when I wondered why my family wasn't like those I saw on television. When I was two, I asked Mother why I did not have a father. She dutifully rang him up and arranged for us to meet. Afterwards, she asked me what I thought, recording the response in her diary with some amusement.

'Didn't like him,' I told her, 'Don't want him.'

It's often said that boys raised by single mothers lament the absence of a paternal figure. I don't recall feeling this way. On the contrary, my curiosity slaked, I forgot the subject almost entirely. For Mother, I think, it had a greater symbolic impact. She was approaching her thirtieth birthday, the undisputed head of her own household. When she was dying, she told me, 'They said I could never have you. But you were the best thing

I ever created.' It was an interesting way of putting it. I got the impression she thought of me in much the same way God thought of Adam.

10

> People are fulfilled only to the extent that they create their world (which is a human world), and create it with their transforming labour. The fulfilment of humankind as human beings lies, then, in the fulfilment of the world. — Paulo Freire

Mother was now approaching her thirtieth birthday. Her doctors conceded she would probably live into middle age, and so she lifted her gaze to the years ahead. The first step she took was to fall in love with Rammy, who appears in our old photo albums looking much as I remember her: clad in Bonds singlets and blue jeans, or sometimes in a state of comic undress, naked from the waist down, wearing her underpants like a hat.

Rammy was both the least appropriate of my mother's lovers, and the only one the rest of the family truly liked. Early in their relationship, she baked a batch of biscuits, laced heavily with marijuana. Unaware of their key ingredient, Mother ate several and became foggy. She thought a cold shower would clear her head, but became lost in the bathroom for the better part of twenty minutes. Afterwards, still sobering up, she and Rammy had a heated discussion as to whether the incident was funny or not.

My family were all teetotallers but, when Mother discussed the biscuits with my grandmother, Gran agreed it was actually quite comical. After the tumultuous years leading up to my birth, I think Rammy's good humour was a source of relief and her vices were forgiven. Mother thought she was wonderful. She had the same boyish charm as my father, but none of his dull conventionality.

They were together when I was learning to speak, and Rammy took an active interest in teaching me to swear. I had learned the word duck, and she taught me to replace the 'D' with an 'F'. Later, I learnt the word 'hole' and would wander about the garden finding holes, shoving my finger into them, and gleefully announcing 'Hole!' Rammy was beside herself with glee. Mother disapproved, but still found it entertaining.

Unfortunately, as my vocabulary improved, my melancholic nature became ever more obvious. My first word was 'No.' My first full sentence was a lament that I had been bitten on the knee by an ant, quickly followed by the phrase, 'I don't want to!' I spoke with enough fluency to complain but not to converse. Mother was disappointed, writing in her diary:

> He's too big to carry about, but too small to keep up. He complains all the time. I love him, but I'm getting bored and want adult company. I think it's time I went back to work, and I think he needs to start mixing with children his own age.'

During my infancy, she had taken maternity leave but now took a second step towards her future, accepting a part-time position teaching junior primary students.

I was duly enrolled in the Teacher's College crèche three days a week, where she hoped I would learn to play with other children and adopt a more upbeat outlook on life. For both of us, the changes proved harder than she had expected.

On her return to work, she found the common attitude to working mothers was no more positive than the attitude to single mothers. She faced a good deal of disapproval from both her fellow teachers and some of the parents. She also had a number of rather unpleasant run-ins with male colleagues who held a strange belief that single mothers were inherently promiscuous. Although she kept her sexuality a secret, and stocked up on floral shirts, they could still tell she was different.

To her worries, I added my own. Each morning, when she dropped me at crèche, I would burst into tears. I would continue weeping until snacks were served at eleven, take a nap, and spend the rest of the day sitting by myself in morose contemplation.

'Don't you want to play with the other boys and girls?' she asked me. 'No,' I would reply.

'But why not?'

'I don't like them.'

Again, Mother was disappointed. She blamed my grandmother, viewing my anti-social outlook as a sort of hereditary trait. In an effort to counteract it, she purchased a children's book called *Leo the Late Bloomer*, following the adventures of a small, inept tiger cub. While the other infant animals in the jungle enjoy normal educational development, Leo spends most of the book mooning about among the flowers. Eventually, through the patience and love of his mother, he experiences an intellectual renaissance that makes the other animals look primitive by comparison. Mother read this book to me hundreds of times. I liked the pictures but didn't really engage with the message.

I preferred the Meg and Mog books, a series of illustrated tales about the adventures of a witch called Meg, her pet cat Mog, and their friend Owl. There are, as I remember it, no other characters. Most of the stories centre around the three of them making magic potions, which backfire with hilarious results.

One night, while Mother was on the phone to a friend, I launched into a game of Meg and Mog, clambered up into the medicine cabinet, and secured a bottle of cough syrup. I used this as a substitute for magic potion, drinking its entire contents. Mother found me giggling to myself, and hallucinating wildly.

She rushed me to hospital, ravished by guilt. 'All the nurses were looking at me like I'd deliberately given you LSD. I felt terrible.'

Aside from the growing rhetoric of conservative 'family values', there was a school of popular psychology devoted to blaming mothers for everything from schizophrenia to autism. The basic hypothesis was that mothers who worked, divorced, or had a life beyond the home were denying their children love, and would spawn a generation of neurotics. Like the medical mythology around homosexuals, these theories have been disproven. At the time I did little to counter them. I was a nervous, recalcitrant little boy.

Still, Mother liked working. Had she been born a decade later, I suspect she would have gone into some other profession but teaching became her vocation. She took great pride in it. She wanted to teach children they need not conform or be dull. Her classrooms were devoid of rote learning and colouring-in exercises, and focused heavily on instilling a sense of agency and a capacity for critical thought. Naturally, her more conservative colleagues took issue with this, but she took their grumbling as an affirmation she was making her mark.

However, as she settled into working life, and grew more sure of herself, I grew more despondent. In the mornings, when she prepared me for crèche, I would mournfully announce, 'I wish I was dead!' I've no idea where I picked this up but the effect was, initially, very successful. Mother was mortified, and would lavish me with gifts in an attempt at consolation.

I liked her response and started to employ the phrase more frequently. If I wanted some new toy while we were out shopping, I would announce I had lost my will to live. One morning I used it because I was upset about the volume of milk on my cereal. Mother finally snapped, thrust me into a cold shower and screamed 'This is what death feels like!' I never used it again, although my mood remained unchanged.

Looking back at it, I know these sorts of incidents could be read as evidence she was a bad mother. Over the years, I've often felt tacitly encouraged to blame her, or my upbringing, for the travails of my own life. Particularly after my father's death, various school counsellors were keen to draw the connection. As an adult, I once saw a psychologist who was confused Mother hadn't passed her homosexuality on to me. 'You were never taught how to be a man,' they told me, 'It must have been very hard to learn it all by yourself?'

I don't think the children of heterosexuals get asked these sorts of questions, although there's certainly a tendency to look at one's mother as a source of one's problems. Bruno Bettelheim, who popularised the theory mothers were responsible for their children's autism, explained the logic by writing:

> It is enough that the infant be convinced that his life is run by insensitive, irrational powers who have complete control over his life and death. Infantile autism is a state of mind that develops in reaction to feeling oneself in an extreme situation, entirely without hope.

The crux of his argument is that mothers are personally responsible for their children's sense of uncontrolled hopelessness. The counterpoint, which seems obvious to me, is that no amount of motherly love will overcome the hardships of poverty and bigotry.

Still, I can see Bettelheim's appeal, and why it took so long before his theories were discredited. Blaming one's mother is a way of dividing one's personality into a combination of 'nature' vs 'nurture'. The good parts one can claim as native to oneself, while the bad parts are assigned to maternal failings. Would I have been a better, or happier, child if my mother hadn't admitted to her homosexuality, or hadn't worked? Would I be a happier, or better, man?

Mother had a friend who had accepted the criticism of working mothers, and devoted her time exclusively to her two daughters. She too was a single parent, and their father was entirely absent. I remember visiting them in their Housing Trust maisonette in the outer suburbs. The house was dominated by a huge mound of board games piled in the living room, all gleaned from local second-hand stores. There was no furniture, except for a table and some old mattresses. The place was rank with a palpable feeling of helplessness.

'I often used to think about her, when we were having a hard time,' Mother once told me. 'When you become a mother, you're encouraged to blame everything on yourself. I think she thought being a single mother meant being a failure, and it became a self-fulfilling prophecy. Working and raising you was difficult, but it was better than being helpless.'

The early eighties was a popular time for these sorts of quasi-rational biases. It wasn't just the legacy of people like Dr Bettelheim, and nor were single parents or homosexuals the only targets. These were the days in which Margaret Thatcher had proclaimed:

> And, you know, there's no such thing as society. There are individual men and women and there are families. And no government can do anything except through people, and people must look after themselves first.

I suppose it's nicer to think that poverty and misfortune are life choices, rather than something that might affect any of us unexpectedly. It makes the fortunate feel their fortune is well earned, and lays blame for misery solely on those experiencing it.

In my late youth, when I was worried about being poor and unemployed, I would often list my various failings and consider who was responsible. Was I faulty because my mother had failed to nurture me correctly? Or was it my fault? Had I not worked hard enough? Was I too weak?

Later, as an undergraduate, I formed an enthusiasm for socialism, and began blaming things on the rich. They were, I argued, rich at the expense of the poor. I thought my mother would appreciate the sentiment but, to my surprise, she ignored it and launched into an attack on my use of collective nouns.

'Which poor people? Which rich people? Name them', she announced.

I found it confusing, because most of my youthful socialist rhetoric was borrowed from her, and I had hoped for her approval.

'You're reducing the structural to the individual. It's just Thatcher's argument in reverse. It sounds good, but it's stupid.'

It took me years to understand the point she was trying to make.

Ironically, it was a way of thinking she'd honed because of me. When I was aged about eighteen months, she had taken me to a dinner party with a group of her lesbian friends. I had thrown a tantrum, and one of them had told her this was indicative of the link between masculinity and violence. 'All men are rapists', they recited.

Mother took offense. 'That's silly,' she told them, 'it's the same as those people who think all homosexuals are immoral, or all women need a man. You can't just take a whole bunch of individuals and say they're all the same.'

I was well into adulthood before I understood her. We were having dinner, and I asked her if she thought people were inherently good or evil. I forget the context of the conversation, but I remember the answer.

'Do you think of yourself as being inherently good or evil?' she asked me.

I thought about it for some minutes. 'Well, I guess I try to be good but it depends a bit on the circumstances.'

'Think about it in more specific terms,' she asked me, 'This afternoon at 4:30, were you being good or evil?'

At 4:30 that afternoon I had been waiting for a bus. I had

been feeling neither good nor evil. 'I was just waiting for the bus,' I told her. I couldn't understand the point she was trying to make.

'So were you being good or evil by waiting for the bus?' she continued, pressing her point, 'Do you think it was society's fault you were waiting for the bus, or was it more of a personal fault? Do you think it was because you're complicit with patriarchy? Is that why you were waiting for the bus?'

'The question doesn't make any sense. I don't understand the point you're trying to make.'

She looked smug. 'Exactly,' she said, and the conversation suddenly ended.

Her logic relied on deliberately confusing the universal and the particular.

In her own life, she had been ascribed so many collective nouns — as an invalid, a single mother, lesbian, poor, working class — that she knew none of them were all-encompassing.

It was not a logic that endeared her to her radical friends, who said she had grown too materialistic. Certainly, her return to work, coupled with taking care of me, drew her away from the reading groups, meetings, and lectures on feminist theory she had previously attended. In her diary she wrote:

> I became aware that many of these women, who dressed like they were poor, experimented with new living methods, and told the system to go jump, had very nice homes to run back to, parents with money to rescue them, and inheritances for their old age. That is not to say they're weren't sincere, but their poverty was a novelty.

> A burnt out, working-class woman has no means of economic support other than the dole, perhaps sickness benefits, or dependency on a husband's income. I could never accept a return to poverty and discomfort, or the powerlessness of being without credit.

At the start of that summer, as I approached my second birthday, her divorce from my father was finalised, and she received a payment from the sale of their house. With this, and the pay slips from her job, she convinced the bank to give her a mortgage. She used it to buy the house in Flinders Park, where I grew up, and in which she lived until she died. It was the third, and largest, step she made to secure our future.

The event appears in her diary as series of mortgage repayment calculations. She estimated she would be in debt until her sixties and, indeed, she never fully paid if off. Our house was one of dozens she looked at, all on the edge of her price range, all uninspiring: stand-alone brick rectangles on wilfully bland streets in dubious suburbs. She chose it because it had superb, mineral-rich soil, so she felt she could at least take comfort in the garden.

We moved in the day before I turned two. It remains one of my earliest memories; I recall us pulling up at the curb with my grandfather and a trailer full of our possessions. While he and my mother wrestled with the refrigerator, I was given sofa cushions to carry indoors. In her diary, Mother wrote that the sense of responsibility with which I shouldered my cushions was very touching.

'I wanted you to have a home,' she later told me, 'I wanted you to feel stable, and not worry that you might be uprooted every time the landlord wanted to up the rent.'

Throughout my childhood, the combination of mortgage and childcare fees consumed the bulk of her income, and our financial circumstances were markedly constrained. However, within the confines of our house and garden, we were isolated and self-sufficient. I knew other people lived differently, but I thought of their lives in purely abstract terms, just as one might imagine life in a different age.

11

> The main idea is that even as we must fully comprehend the pastness of the past, there is no just way in which the past can be quarantined from the present.
> — Edward Said

On our first night in Flinders Park, Mother was visited by a ghost. The ghost took the form of an old lady, who stood in the doorway to the bedroom, peering at her nervously as she was settling into bed. She assumed it was the spirit of the previous owner and, after several silent minutes, decided she should speak to it. 'It will be all right,' she told the ghost, 'We will take care of the house now.' The ghost nodded and disappeared. Mother turned out the light and went to sleep.

The encounter was surprising, partly because my mother did not believe in ghosts, but also because ghosts are usually associated with places where something significant has happened: castles, battle fields, old manors, and the former abodes of the great and the good. Mother asked one of our neighbours if anything significant had occurred in our house. They looked at her like she was mad.

'No, of course not,' they told her.

'What happened to the previous owner?' she asked.

'She died last year. They found her in her chair, in front of the TV.'

I had my own, less mystical, sources of concern. Both

the house and garden were much larger than our previous maisonette and I was terrified of getting lost along the long hallway separating the kitchen from the bedrooms, or in the vast expanses of the yard. I thought a monstrous lion lived in the drains, roaring with rage whenever we emptied the bathtub. I was worried it would break free and eat us. Mother assured me this was not very likely but I did not believe her.

Even after I overcame these fears, Flinders Park remained an unsettling place to live. It had been built on a flood plain and was unrelentingly flat. There were no changes in contour and the streets were all uniform, laid out in grids, lined with houses of the same vintage, fabric, and dimensions. There was no town centre, and we hardly ever saw anyone outdoors.

The only landmark was a narrow and sickly river, running past the end of our street. Along its banks, a poorly maintained path meandered through a narrow band of scrub. We walked our dogs there, occasionally running into other dog walkers or petty drug dealers, whom Mother would try to engage in conversation.

When we first moved in, she had hoped the river would provide something comparable to the gully she had played in as a girl; a place in which I might wander, free and happy. In fairness, the lack of regular maintenance did lend it an invitingly wild aura. The banks were lined with she-oaks and gums. Reeds and bone weed clustered at the water's edge, and small groups of ducks floated about on the surface. Sometimes we would see people fishing, but all they caught were huge, copper-coloured carp. As these were inedible, they would be left to rot on the banks.

It was, however, not really a river but a vast drain, dug out during the Great Depression, mostly to provide work for the unemployed. Before that, the area had been reed beds and wetlands. Afterwards, it was re-zoned for housing. Most of the water in the river was run-off from the local roads and, where it grew still, one could make out the sheen of automotive oil.

Sometimes, after heavy rain, it would flood dramatically, and Mother and I would stand on the footbridge at the end of the street and watch it raging below. When the waters settled, we would walk along the banks, inspecting the damage. The high-water mark would be mapped out by plastic bags, caught in the branches of low hanging trees. These would remain, dangling like mistletoe, until the next flood.

When we first moved in Mother allowed me to play on the banks, and in the river itself. This did not last long, nor end well. Clambering through the shallows one day, a piece of glass become lodged in my foot. At that age, I devoted so much time to complaining that my mother didn't realise I had an actual, rather than imagined, injury for almost two weeks. By then, the shard of glass had burrowed in so deeply it had to be surgically removed. Mother was wracked with guilt, which I milked for all it was worth.

After that, we began to visit one of the neighbourhood's few playgrounds. It consisted of a set of monkey bars, a dented slippery dip, and a concrete tunnel, set up next to the carpark by the local football oval. The centrepiece of the playground, however, was a replica of the Endeavour, the boat upon which James Cook first arrived in Australia in 1770.

It wasn't a very accurate replica, being much smaller than the original and built of treated pine logs. A small plaque, attached to the hull, announced that it had been installed in 1970 to mark the bicentenary of Cook's foray into Botany Bay. By the time I first stepped aboard, the wood was splintering badly and the deck awash with empty chip packets and cigarette butts. It was less dangerous than the river but far more depressing.

After I moved to Sydney, I often heard people use the word 'suburban' as a synonym for bland normality. It's not an idea I disagree with, but I think it underestimates the uncanny aura that permeates the post-war suburb. The French philosopher Paul Virilio articulates it well:

> Francis Fukuyama was wrong in predicting the end of history… The question is not the end of history but the end of geography.

He wasn't writing specifically about suburbs, but he captures how I remember Flinders Park. It seemed beyond any common notion of geography. Nothing in particular stood out, and its extreme flatness gave it a sense of running on, unbroken, forever.

After a week or two, I lost interest in the Endeavour, and we began to spend more and more of our time at home or, more specifically, in the garden. When we first moved in, it was indiscernible from its neighbours, consisting of patchy grass, a few sickly ornamentals, and some malnourished fruit trees. Within a year, it had begun to attain the magical aura I still associate with it.

Each weekend we visited the hardware store to buy bags of potting soil, or patrolled school fetes in search of cheap plants. When we got home, Mother would stride about with her shovel, jamming shrubs into the earth or prodding at mounds of manure and pea straw. For the first year, she ignored the lawn as best she could, and spent her time lavishing liquid fertilisers upon the trees. These included a fragrant crab apple by the front fence and a lemon myrtle overhanging the letter box, both overshadowed by a towering flame tree. An avenue of pussy willow grew over the driveway, leading to two bitter apple trees in front of the shed.

On the other side of the house, in a lightless patch between my bedroom window and the neighbour's fence, stood a mature apricot of considerable size. Its growth seemed an anomaly until we found its roots were clogged deep into the plumbing system. Each summer it produced a blizzard of apricots and made the side path inaccessible.

By the back veranda there was a fig tree and a mandarin and, at the very rear of the yard, two aging plum trees. Beneath these we buried our beloved cats, dogs and other assorted pets over the years. Thus fuelled, the trees produced prolific supplies of fruit.

The garden's centrepiece, however, was a peach tree, growing in the very middle of the back garden. It was upon this that Mother devoted her most intoxicating manures. After I moved out, it fruited so copiously it cracked a branch and became infected with some sort of parasite. When she rang to tell me the news she was forlorn. She had been enjoying fresh peaches for years and forgotten how supermarket fruit paled by comparison.

Around the trees, she scattered nasturtium seeds, taken from my grandparents' garden. Each summer, they unleashed a horde of huge green leaves, smothering the lawn and any weaker shrubs. When they died back in autumn, she dug up the withered remnants of lawn and laid down beds of manure and pea straw.

In winter, she dragged bags of soil into the living room so she could pot up seedlings in front of the electric heater, where it was warm. After a year or two, the carpets were ruined, but each spring she had a mass of seedlings ready to be jammed back into the earth, along with another dose of manure and a scattering of nasturtium seeds. She repeated this cycle yearly until, after six or seven years, there was no lawn left.

A few cleared patches were maintained for more practical plants, mostly scented herbs and vegetables. As she hated both kitchens and cooking, she grew food we could eat without preparation: snow peas, broad beans, cherry tomatoes, and smaller varieties of zucchini. She would graze on these while gardening, thus avoiding the need to enter the kitchen for days at a time.

The growth of the garden made it stand out among the neighbourhood, but it also created a physical barrier, isolating us from our neighbours. We would occasionally hear the sound of their lawn mowers, or someone with their television turned up, but otherwise it was as if they didn't exist. Sometimes, I would climb the flame tree in our front yard, up above the canopy of the smaller trees and undergrowth, and look out over the suburb. It was like being in the crow's nest of a ship, marooned in a vast and unremarkable sea.

Over time, her garden became a suburban landmark. When she grew old, and attained the revered status of neighbourhood eccentric, people would stop her in the street to talk about it, or ask for gardening tips. Once, flying home to visit her, the plane banked before landing and I saw our house from the air. It stood out like a great plume of green, jutting out from the flat, baked, quarter-acre blocks surrounding it.

My mother would not have admitted it, but I think our house mimicked that of her own childhood home. She had grown up on the top of a hill, detached from the city and surrounded by forest. Now, she had created her own forest, and its density isolated us from the suburb surrounding us. I played in her garden much as she had once played in the gully. The primary difference was that she had believed the outside world promised something wonderful, whereas I thought it was all one dull, unending, and slightly menacing mass.

12

The child and the adult live in different worlds.
— George Orwell

For my third birthday, Mother gave me a small toy bear. I named him Tubby. The two of us quickly became inseparable. On weekends, we would take a pair of secateurs and carve out a clearing in the garden, where we played together in contented seclusion. In spring and summer, when the weather was good, we usually stayed outdoors all day.

During the working week, my life was less idyllic. Each morning, as Mother readied herself for work and me for crèche, I would beg to be left at home. After she dropped me off, Tubby and I kept to ourselves as best we could. I vividly remember us playing on a slippery dip, surrounded by other children who we pointedly ignored. Afterwards, we had our afternoon snack and sat by the front door for three hours, waiting for Mother to pick us up.

I tried to reassure Tubby that we would soon be back in the garden. 'She won't be much longer,' I told him. He looked up at me, forlornly. 'Not long now and we can go home.'

When Mother arrived, the manager took her into the office, where they had a cup of tea and a long conversation, while I waited outside. They must have been discussing me as, the next morning, Mother suggested I leave Tubby at home. 'You could play with the other boys and girls instead?'

'No,' I told her. 'But why not?'

'I only want to play with Tubby.'

She had been reading me *Leo the Late Bloomer* every night for almost a year without any apparent improvement. On the contrary, I was growing ever more reclusive and recalcitrant, and she grew ever more frustrated. Naturally, she blamed my grandmother. 'He's inherited this from you,' she told Gran.

'You can't blame me,' Gran argued, 'If he doesn't want to play with the other children, I don't see why he should.'

'The manager at the crèche thinks he needs to learn to socialise, or he'll have trouble once he starts primary school. She says he's like a hermit. He just sits around talking to his bear all day.'

'If the other children can't compete with a stuffed toy bear then they're probably just very dull. I never told you who to play with, did I? And you turned out all right.'

I was allowed to continue taking Tubby to crèche, but Mother was not happy about it. She decided that our family was unhealthily anti-social, which was probably true. 'You take after your grandmother,' she used to tell me, 'I'm the only one with any social skills. It's like the misanthrope gene skipped a generation.'

Yet Mother had her own isolationist tendencies. After we moved to Flinders Park she began a second affair, this time with a woman named Francine. It was unfashionably heteronormative to insist on monogamy, but Rammy was clearly upset. Much like Mother's tumultuous liaisons with my father and June, or June and the ill-fated Alice, managing two relationships simultaneously had the effect of asserting her commitment to neither.

A few months before my fourth birthday, Mother wrote, 'Feel a bit sad and lonely. Wish someone else was here,' but when Rammy tried to visit she sent her away. She complained of their relationship, 'Lots of assertion, explanation, communication needed.' Shortly afterwards, she decided to embark on a period of celibacy. I have no idea what either Rammy or Francine made of this. Mother did not document the end of either relationship. Their names simply disappear from her diaries.

By the time I turned four she was single again and we were on our own. She did not have another relationship for another fourteen years. I assume she got lonely. Certainly, I was no replacement for adult company. Her diaries detail my various failures, and the concerns they caused her. I was, she wrote, painfully shy, afraid of virtually everything, and only seemed happy when I was trekking about the garden with Tubby. 'Soon he will have to start school,' she wrote, 'How will he cope? He is utterly socially inept.'

In an effort to improve my social skills, she sought out friends with children and arranged a series of play dates. These were uniformly unsuccessful. They usually began with me sitting beneath my mother's chair while she tried to talk to her friends, and ending when I started sobbing and begged to be taken home. 'He makes himself a natural target for mockery,' she lamented in her diary, 'When I make him play with other children, he just stands about looking pompous. When they make fun of him, he bursts into tears.'

After a while, Mother ran out of friends willing to endure the spectacle of my weeping. She was obliged to consider other options. My grandmother suggested I might benefit from a pet. She thought it would encourage me to engage with other living things, and draw me out of my fantasy world. 'You and your siblings all had pets,' Gran told her, 'It's good for a child to have a pet to take care of.'

Mother and her siblings had grown up with a menagerie of dogs, cats, birds, rodents, and, on one occasion, a foul smelling but cheerful ferret. 'You had that nice little terrier,' Gran reminded my mother, 'She made you focus on yourself a bit less.'

Mother duly obtained a ginger kitten, who I imaginatively named Ginger. He quickly grew into a huge, vicious tom cat. Initially, I thought cats were a bit like living teddy bears; I remember rushing to gather him up in a warm embrace only to have him dig his claws deep into my face. From this, I learned I could only relate to Ginger if I placed his agency on par with my own. Every time I forgot this lesson, he would forcibly remind me.

Ginger spent most of his days stalking around the garden until he found some warm and secluded spot to doze. He did not want to play with other cats or go anywhere. When he wasn't either asleep or butchering smaller animals, he sat in the low hanging boughs of trees and took swipes at those passing below. I thought he was brilliant and did my best to emulate him.

At four and a half, I experienced a growth spurt whereby my tongue grew faster than my mouth. This left me with a terrible lisp, and an inability to pronounce the letter 'n'. As a result, I could not pronounce my own name. 'Iatho', I would mumble, looking at my feet. Mother had given me an unusual name in the hope that it would fuel my sense of individuality. She now feared it had become a curse. I burst into tears every time I was introduced to anyone new.

In the weeks before I started primary school, she booked an appointment with the principal, and arranged a tour of the classrooms. She hoped this would familiarise me with the school grounds, and make both of us feel more comfortable. 'We're going to go and see the school for big kids,' she explained.

I remember the visit clearly. We met the principal, who must have sensed Mother's nerves as she made a number of reassuring comments. 'It's very normal for children to feel a bit nervous when they start school but they soon settle in.'

'He's not very social, and he has a hard time making friends,' Mother explained.

'He seems like a very nice little boy,' replied the principle, and then turned to me, 'I'm sure you and I will be the very best of friends, won't we?'

I thought it was a strange thing to say, given the disparity in our ages, but I was comforted to think I would have a friend to play with. She seemed, I thought, quite nice. Mother and I visited one of the classrooms, where we met my future teacher, and some of the children in the year above me.

This did not go so well. At that point, I had a deep attachment to a small pink plastic pony. Mother had convinced me to leave Tubby in the car, but I had insisted on taking the pony with me. When I entered the classroom, clutching it to my chest, I became the object of unwanted attention.

While Mother introduced herself to the teacher, a group of boys sitting at the back of the room began yelling at me. 'Look! He's got a pony!' yelled one.

'It's pink!' yelled another.

They burst into a chorus of riotous laughter, and the teacher quickly ushered us out of the room. This, I think, was my first unhappy run-in with the conventions of masculinity.

I don't think it went well for Mother either. She had raised the topic of before and after school care, and the teacher told her, in no uncertain terms, that these options did not exist. Asked about her curriculum, the teacher explained she had a series of colouring-in sheets themed around the letters of the alphabet, and another set focused on basic arithmetic.

As the start of the school year grew near, Mother grew progressively more anxious. A week before classes started, she took me to see the film *The Neverending Story*, in which a small boy, persecuted by local bullies, takes solace in a book about a mythical world. In this world, a mysterious force called 'the Nothingness', fed by the power of human fear, is slowly destroying the world. To defeat it, a boy warrior is sent upon a great quest, in which he must draw upon the strength of his own character.

At one point, the Nothingness drowns the boy warrior's horse in a swamp, but he struggles on regardless. At the film's conclusion, this fable inspires the small boy to close the book, stand up to his bullies, and confront his fears.

'Did you like it?' Mother asked me afterwards. 'Yes I did.'

'It was good, wasn't it? It was about a little boy who needed to be brave, wasn't it?'

'No, it wasn't.'

'What did you think it was about?'

'It was about a boy who runs away from some bullies, and spends a day by himself.'

'What about the bit where he confronts his fears and faces the Nothingness?'

'That's when the boy warrior's horse drowns in the mud.'

We discussed it again a week later, on the morning of my first day at school, as she packed my bag and checked on the contents of my lunch box.

'Can I take Tubby with me,' I asked.

'No, I think Tubby needs to stay home. He might get lost.'

'Can I stay home?'

'No, you need to go to school. That's where big boys go. Don't you want to be a big boy?'

'No, I do not! I am afraid and I want to stay home!'

'You need to conquer your fear. Remember in the film? You need to fight the Nothingness.'

I took up a length of garden hose, rushed out into the front yard, and began to wave the hose about in mock combat. Mother told me this wasn't enough. She bundled me into the car, and we drove off to school.

When we arrived, the school ground was empty. My friend the principal was nowhere to be seen. Mother had taken up a full-time job at another school a few suburbs away, and needed to hurry off to her own classroom.

'We're a bit early,' Mother told me, 'but let's go find your teacher and say good morning.'

We went to my classroom, where my teacher was sorting through a pile of colouring-in books. 'Can I leave him with you?' asked Mother.

'No, I'm very busy,' said the teacher, 'and class doesn't start for another half an hour.'

'I know, but I need to go to work.'

The teacher scowled at her. 'I suppose he can wait in the hallway.'

We went into the hallway, where Mother checked my

lunchbox again, and handed me my school bag. 'Now,' she explained, 'you need to be a good boy and wait here for a few minutes before your class starts.'

'But I don't want to,' I protested.

'I know, but I need to go to work, so you just need to wait here for a little bit.'

Thus began the ritual with which I filled our mornings for the first three months of my education. Each day, Mother would deposit me outside my classroom and I would stand, frozen with terror, watching her walk away. After several horrified minutes, I would burst in to tears and run screaming through the halls until, eventually, one of the teachers noticed me, and dragged me back to my classroom. Mother was right; I was unprepared for school.

13

> [I]n the child's progress through school, we shall recognise the history of the cultural development of the world traced, as it were, in a silhouette.
> — G. W. F. Hegel

When I think back to my first weeks at school, I mostly remember the playground. It was a barren field, punctuated by withered shrubs and battered play equipment. Its centrepiece was a sort of bunker, made of four concrete pipes, dug into the earth, and leading into a large pit.

One lunch time, while standing on the edge of this pit, I saw a boy throw a rock at another boy's head. I don't think he did it intentionally. I had been watching him and I think he was just throwing rocks for the sheer joy of it. Most fell harmlessly about the playground, but inevitably one found a target. I heard a faint thudding noise, followed by a panicked cry for help. 'My head! My head! Help me! I'm dying!'

The victim was a blonde-headed boy from my class. A small crowd gathered around him. As I watched, I could see a bloom of blood appear above his ear. A third boy, a little older than the rest, inspected his wound. His face turned white, and he suddenly recoiled. 'Someone get a teacher! His head is bleeding!'

There were no teachers to be seen, and we all stood, frozen. I felt sure the boy would die. The rock throwing boy stood by, nonplussed, still holding a handful of pebbles. I tried to explain the gravity of the situation to him. 'He's going to die!'

He laughed, casually threw a rock into the dust, and walked away. I was shocked, and I ran off to hide behind some bushes at the edge of the playground. I don't know what happened to the injured boy.

After that, I spent my recess and lunch breaks wandering alone by the basketball courts on the edge of the playground, or hiding behind the bushes. I tried to stay as far away from the other children as possible. Mostly I succeeded, but on one occasion, a teacher came up to me, dragging another small boy behind him. 'You're not playing with the others,' he told me. I couldn't tell if it was a question or an observation, so I stood there, gaping at him.

'You two are going to play together.'

He pushed the other boy towards me and walked away. The boy immediately began to speak to himself in gibberish, and then abruptly ran off. I stayed where I was, knowing I was obliged to obey the teacher but unsure how. A few minutes later the teacher reappeared, looking irate. 'You're not playing with the other boy,' he said.

He grabbed my hand, and dragged me over to the bunker, where a boy from the year above me was standing by himself, scratching the ground with a piece of stick. 'You two are going to play together,' the teacher repeated, and then strode off towards the staff room.

Unlike his predecessor, my new playmate was suspiciously excited to meet me. He inducted me into a game which involved poking at the ground with sticks and running about. It had no discernible logic but I did my best to follow the teacher's orders. When the bell rang for the end of lunch, the boy declared we would ignore it. 'We don't want to go inside and play their stupid games, do we?'

I thought he had a good point. I didn't want to go back into the classroom. 'Let's stay out here,' he suggested. 'We can keep playing our own games until it's time to go home.'

I thought this sounded reasonable. The teacher had, after all, instructed us to play together. We continued poking at the ground with our sticks. Soon we were the only ones left on the playground. It was, I thought, a much nicer place without all the other children.

Soon the teacher returned, told us we had broken the rules, and dragged us back to class. I had no idea what rule I'd broken. I was told to play with the other boy, and that was what I had done. I felt a deep sense of injustice. Shortly afterwards I wet myself. I knew there was a toilet down the hall from my classroom, and that there were rules involved in accessing it, but had no idea what those rules were. Instead, I sat in my shame, until the teacher noticed my quiet sobbing and ushered me out of the room.

I experienced lots of problems with the school toilets. I had always followed Mother into the Ladies and had never been into a male public toilet by myself, certainly not one frequented by small boys. I found them very confronting. Early on, I walked into a cubical, where I discovered a pair of underpants filled with poo. I suppose the owner had been shocked by what he'd done and abandoned them. I was horrified.

I found the urinals especially mortifying. The spectacle of that sheer wall of metal, draining into a piss-filled trough, struck me as barbaric. I didn't understand how they were supposed to be used so, rather than simply lowering my fly when I urinated,

I dropped my pants around my ankles. Sometime at the start of Term Two, I discovered this was a serious faux pas.

I had gone into a cubical when I heard some older boys enter the toilet and gather around the urinal, talking and laughing loudly. I was surprised to hear them mention my name. 'Have you seen how he drops his pants all the way down when he does a wee?' one of them said.

They were, I realised, unaware of my presence.

'He's a sissy!' said another.

'Let's wait till he does a wee, and then laugh at him!'

'Let's steal his trousers!'

I was mortified, and remained cowering in the cubical until I was confident they had left. I vowed never again to use the school toilets.

Throughout my entire education, I remained true to this vow. Through both primary and high school, it was only under the utmost duress that I entered the toilet block. Weeks would pass when, through limited fluid intake and careful diet, I avoided making use of the school's facilities.

As the weeks wore on, my classmates pointed out other mistakes I was making. For Mother's Day, we were instructed to draw a portrait of our mothers, and I drew what I felt to be quite an accurate image. I depicted Mother in her garden, with her dungarees and short hair.

'That's not a mother,' one girl told me, 'Mothers have long hair and a dress. You're meant to draw your mother.'

'But that's what my mother looks like,' I protested.

'No it's not. You're meant to draw your mother.'

Our classmates gathered around until begrudgingly I took a brown pencil and extended Mother's hair. I refused to add a dress. It was after that I stopped calling her 'Mum' or 'Mummy', and started saying 'Mother.' I thought it sounded more definite, formal, and harder for anyone to argue with.

Despite compromising on my Mother's Day portrait, I was still subject to regular criticism. There seemed to be no sphere of schoolyard life I could negotiate without disgracing myself. Even ostensibly enjoyable activities were opportunities for humiliation. For every game of Tunnel Ball, Red Rover, and Heads Down Thumbs Up I pretended to understand the rules, only to endure the ire of my classmates when it became obvious I did not. I was nearly always the last to be chosen for any team, preferred only occasionally over another boy who had asthma and feet so flat he could barely run.

Briefly, I befriended a small girl, with whom I spent a few happy lunch breaks building tiny houses out of twigs. Mother thought this was a good sign, and arranged play dates. I went to her house after school and, once or twice, she visited ours. Soon I discovered our friendship was another faux pas.

'You play with girls!' one of the boys in our class told me. He seemed angry. 'Boys don't play with girls. You love her. You want to marry her. It makes me want to be sick.'

Later, her parents discovered my mother was a homosexual. I don't know how. The girl was prohibited from playing at our house although I was unaware of this at the time. Mother told me years later. 'They said they weren't comfortable with her coming to our house. I think they thought I'd molest her.'

By the mid-year break, I still had no friends. I often missed Tubby but had decided the school yard was no place for a teddy bear. I was worried he would feel rejected. 'I want to take you with me,' I explained, 'but it's too dangerous. The other children are very scary, and they might hurt you.'

I longed for Tubby's company so badly I believed we could communicate telepathically. As I wandered the playground alone, I would speak to him and ask for his advice. 'There's a group of older boys throwing sticks. I'm worried I'll get hit in the eye.'

'Don't run!' he would tell me, 'That will only make you an appealing target. Walk in the other direction as calmly as you can.'

Mother found it hard. She had loved school and hoped I would do the same. As I struggled along, she felt a mixture of guilt at her inability to protect me and intense frustration at my lack of stoicism.

Other, more material concerns, weighed upon her. It had been a decade since her transplant, and she was beginning to suffer the side effects. Her kidney medication gave her Cushing's Syndrome, causing her muscles to waste away, and throwing her hormones out of balance. She had previously been willowy and thin, but now developed the physique she later described as a 'pumpkin with sticks for limbs.' Her doctors told her she had contracted Hepatitis C from a poorly screened blood transfusion.

Every few weeks before school, we visited the local hospital where I stood beside her as the nurses took blood samples. In the waiting room, we had our first conversations about her health. 'I have to take the tablets or my kidney will stop working, but the tablets also make me feel a bit sick,' she explained.

'What would happen if you stopped taking the tablets?'

'I would get very sick, and then I would die.'

'What would happen to me?'

'Well, I'm not going to stop taking the tablets, so nothing will change.'

'But what if you did?'

'You would go to live with Gran.'

'And what would happen to Tubby?'

'He would go with you.'

'And what about our house and the garden?'

'I'm not going to die, so you don't need to worry about it.'

Of course, I did worry about it. I imagined myself living in the house in Flinders Park alone. Tubby and I built a series of hideouts at the back of the garden, so we could hide if Mother died and anyone tried to take us away. We stocked them with small packets of breakfast cereal and long-life milk.

Towards the end of the year, the interest rates on Mother's mortgage rose, bringing about a long period of financial insecurity. I remember this because of its effect on the quality of our diet. For several years, we ate mostly white bread smeared with condiments and whatever bounties could be harvested from the garden.

Mother later recalled it as a time of immense stress. 'It was very difficult. We were very poor, and you were not an easy child to raise,' she complained, 'It was like trying to parent a Dickens character.'

'What sort of Dickens character? You mean, like Fagin, or more like Oliver Twist?'

'I used to think I should have called you Little Nell. You were so melancholy it would have been funny if I hadn't had to deal with it every day.'

By the end of the year, financially and emotionally drained, she had reached her wits end. One winter morning before school, I launched into a heartfelt soliloquy on why I should be allowed to stay home, followed by a period of uncontrolled sobbing. 'I didn't have enough money to pay for petrol, and I wasn't sure I'd be able to get to work,' she recalled, 'so I left you weeping into your Weet-bix and went to sit in the garden for a bit to collect my thoughts. And then a funny thing happened.'

Sitting on a bale of pea straw at the very back of the yard beneath the plum trees, she felt a sudden, immense sense of peace. 'I looked up, and it was the Virgin Mary,' floating just above the plum trees.'

'How did you know it was the Virgin Mary?'

'I just knew.'

'What did you do?'

'I told her I appreciated her concern but I wasn't ready for religion at that point.'

'And what did she do?'

'She was very understanding. She smiled and then sort of disappeared. She seemed very nice. Perhaps I'll become a Catholic when I'm older.'

Years later, when she was dying, she assured me she was still an atheist.

After her encounter with the Virgin, Mother told her doctors she was feeling a bit stressed. They referred her to a family psychologist, who we visited three or four times. I spent most of the sessions playing with a toy elephant they kept in their office, but Mother found it useful. She reluctantly admitted she found being a single mother tiring, and sometimes wished I would stop weeping and pull my socks up. To her surprise, the psychologist told her this was quite reasonable.

'You're very poor, you're working full time and it sounds

like you've been a bit unwell lately,' the psychologist observed.

'Yes, that's right.'

'And you also have an extremely strong-willed little boy who does not like going to school, and isn't afraid of telling you so.'

'Do you think I'm depressed?'

'No, I think you're tired.'

'And what about Ianto? Is he depressed?'

'No, he just hates going to school.'

After the first session, the psychologist sent her home with instructions to write out a list of all the things she liked about being a single mother. I found the list in her diary after she died, buried among a series of budgets and shopping lists:

> We belong to each other.
>
> There is no room for any bullshit.
>
> There are no barriers as we have to be totally honest. I like that.
>
> He is one of the few people who wants me to be myself. Not out of love for me but because as an only child of an only parent he is vulnerable and needs to know exactly how things are.

In the second session, they talked about me. Mother did most of the talking, and I sat playing with the toy elephant.

'Some kids just don't like school,' the psychologist said.

'So, what should I do?'

'Send him to school with some toy cars.'

'Do you think that will make him more sociable?'

'No. But it'll help him find some other kids to play with, and he might calm down a bit.'

I was duly sent to school with three Matchbox automobiles. To my surprise, I found myself spending my lunch and recess times with a small group of playmates, pushing toy cars about in the dust behind the basketball courts. I didn't understand the games they were playing, but I came to accept that the spectacle of participation greased the wheels of social interaction, even when it was unclear what I was participating in. Mother was greatly relieved.

14

> Perhaps the oldest and certainly one of the most famous sanctuaries in Greece was that of Dodona, where Zeus was revered in the oracular oak. The thunder-storms which are said to rage at Dodona more frequently than anywhere else in Europe, would render the spot a fitting home for the god whose voice was heard alike in the rustling of the oak leaves and in the crash of thunder. — Sir James George Frazer

All through the autumn months, I took my toy cars to school and, in winter, they bore fruit. I was invited to a birthday party. Mother was delighted. It was the primary topic of conversation at our next visit to the psychologist. 'The toy cars worked! He's been invited to a party!'

I was much less enthused. I accepted that I had to go to school, but did not see why I should have to see my classmates on the weekend.

'He'll probably try to back out of it,' said the psychologist, 'but it's important he goes. Be gentle but firm.'

Of course, I did try to back out of it. On the morning of the party, I was so nervous I could not eat my Weet-bix. Instead, I lay on the kitchen floor, weeping. 'Please! Please! Don't make me go!'

'But you've been playing with the other children at school. This won't be any different. And there'll be a birthday cake.

Won't that be nice?'

The party was only a block away, and Mother and I walked there together, me sobbing and begging, and her being gentle but firm. 'You're going to have a nice time,' she kept repeating.

'No! I won't! I won't have a nice time! I never have a nice time!' Tears streamed down my face, saturating the front of my t-shirt.

Mother marched on resolutely, holding my hand. Halfway there, we found a small metal star laying in the gutter, part of the rusted workings of some long-dismantled household appliance. 'Look! It's a lucky charm. If you keep this in your pocket, you'll have a nice time.'

I looked at the star dubiously but accepted Mother probably knew what she was talking about. Clutching it tightly, I allowed myself to be deposited at the party where, much to my surprise, I did have a nice time. I was given a bag of lollies, a piece of cake, and managed to take part in a series of semi-organised parlour games without crying. Two hours later, when Mother came to collect me, I enthusiastically declared the lucky charm had worked.

'It wasn't the lucky charm,' she proclaimed. 'You did it!' You had a nice time all on your own.'

'No, it was the lucky charm.'

'But it isn't a lucky charm at all! It's just a piece of old metal, probably off an old refrigerator.'

I suppose she thought this would be affirming, but I knew she was wrong. Over the following weeks, I became obsessed with lucky charms. In addition to the metal star, I accumulated an array of other lucky objects: small plastic figurines, the stubs of old pencils, bits of stick, and pebbles. When I escaped a day unscathed, I thanked them. When something went wrong, I assumed one of them had soured from good luck to bad, and fretted over how best to identify and purge it from my collection.

The luckiest of all was a small Garfield statuette, made of soft plastic, purchased from the gift stand at a petrol station. I hadn't seen the Garfield comics, but thought the statuette must be lucky as it resembled my cat, Ginger. I identified its lucky properties early in the summer, during a lunchtime game of cricket.

Cricket was not a sport I enjoyed but I knew non-participation would mark me out for mockery. The other boys were obsessed with it. None of us possessed enough coordination to connect bat and ball, so the matches consisted of long arguments as to who got to bat, who got to bowl, and who got to be the wicket keeper. I spent the time in the outfield, clutching my Garfield statuette, and hoping to be forgotten.

'Please don't let the ball come anywhere near me,' I prayed, rubbing the statuette like a rosary. 'Please don't let them make me bat. Please don't let them make me bowl. Please don't let them make me be the wicket keeper.'

I repeated this mantra to myself every lunch time for about eight weeks, and wore the statuette down to a misshapen orange blob. I never had to bat, bowl, or keep stumps once. The ball never even came near me. Shortly before the end of the year, one boy hit another in the head with a cricket bat and the game was banned outside of official competition. It was, I thought, a miracle. I made a small shrine next to my bed, where I kept the Garfield statuette and the metal star.

Just before the Christmas break, I noticed the Garfield comics in the daily paper. Assuming these were also lucky, I began to study them like scripture.

'What are you doing?' Mother asked me.

'I am reading Garfield.'

'Do you want me to help you read the words?'

'No. I can read them.'

I don't think she believed me. I had been refusing to read along to *Leo the Late Bloomer*, despite her relentless encouragement.

'Really?' Can you tell me what they say?'

'Garfield is telling Pookie he loves him.'

Mother was astounded. She had assumed I was illiterate. She purchased several Garfield compendiums, which I slowly made my way through. At the end of the year, she met with my teacher. 'I think he can read. He's been reading Garfield comics.'

'Yes,' the teacher told her, 'He's reading at the same level as a seven-year-old. Unfortunately, I've had to fail him because his colouring-in skills are terrible, and I don't like his handwriting.'

Mother didn't care. It was, she thought, the first sign I was beginning to bloom. She began looking for more challenging reading material. In the remainder bins at our local newsagent, she found a heavily discounted graphic novel version of Daniel Defoe's *Robinson Crusoe*. I think it must have been published as a way of introducing children to English literature, as it was terribly simplified and only forty pages long.

I thought it was marvellous. 'I like it because he gets to live on his own, and doesn't have to go to school,' I told Mother.

At the start of the summer holidays, Tubby and I built a new fortress in the cornucopia of the garden and resolved to live like Crusoe. We admired his attitude to isolation:

> I am divided from mankind, a solitaire, one banished from human society. But I am not starving and perishing on a barren place, affording no sustenance.

I was alone, but the fruit trees were in bloom and I did not have to go to school for six long and happy weeks. Tubby and I planted a garden, and tried to extract clay out of the soil so we could make pottery.

Mother felt she needed a break. She borrowed a tent from my grandparents and told me we were going on a camping trip. To her surprise, I was quite excited. I thought it sounded like the kind of thing Robinson Crusoe would do. We began at Murray Bridge, so-called because it famously hosts a bridge across its titular river. Mother had spent many of her own school holidays there when she was a girl, holidaying with her family.

When she was in her early teens, my grandfather finished building their house, and turned his attention to the construction of a houseboat. He had no experience with either sailing or building boats, but simply welded together several forty-gallon drums, atop of which he built a small shack. He bolted a motorcycle engine to the back, attached a makeshift propeller, and then borrowed a trailer, carted his contraption to Murray Bridge, and lowered it into the water. To everyone's surprise, it floated. The family spent many happy summers bobbing about on it, until it eventually sank.

So it was that we began our driving holiday at Murray Bridge. We found a camp ground, swam in the river, looked at the bridge, and then visited a small grotto, within which lurked a fibreglass bunyip. If you placed twenty cents into a coin slot built into the grotto's walls, the bunyip rose out of the water emitting a horrible scream and then sank again. 'Are there really bunyips in the river?' I asked Mother.

'No, they're mythological creatures.'

'Where does the river come from?'

She explained it ran all the way from the mountains in New South Wales, and then out into the ocean. That night, as I fell asleep in our tent, I could hear the water lapping against the river bank, ebbing outwards into the mystery of an unknown earth.

Over the following days, we drove from town to town. Each had its own little tourist traps: good bakeries, swimming spots, large fibreglass animals, or historical sites marked out with pieces of outdated agricultural or industrial machinery. In one little town, we found a museum of fossils, gems, and minerals, contained within the home of an amateur geologist. Aside from exhibiting his collection, he also sold off lesser pieces to unwitting tourists. Mother purchased several fossilised shark's teeth, extracted from the limestone banks of the river.

We studied these together and she explained that the entire area had once formed the basin of a vast ocean. I asked where the ocean had gone and she attempted to explain the movement of tectonic plates. Later, we drove through one of the national parks, following an unpaved road through the scrub until we came to a series of sand dunes. There we found mounds of sun-bleached mussel shells.

'Are these fossils as well?' I asked Mother.

'No, these are shells. People used to camp here, and they'd fish the mussels out of the river and then have big parties. But they don't anymore.'

'Why not?'

'Well,' she explained, 'the British came, shot everyone, or made them move away, and then took over the place to graze their sheep.'

There had been, I later learned, a massacre in the early 1840s, just a few miles upstream. We walked on, through the dunes, until we found a creek, clogged with feral willows. We could see carp, flapping about in the shallows.

Mother explained these were a legacy of the same era. 'Willows and carp aren't native. The British introduced them because they thought they'd make the place seem more like Britain.'

'Why did they do that?'

'They thought they were like Robinson Crusoe. They thought they were all alone, so they could do whatever they wanted without hurting anyone.'

'But Robinson Crusoe found those footprints in the sand.'

'Yes, and he made Friday his servant, and shot the islanders, didn't he? He was never really on his own.'

We walked upstream, until we reached a stagnant and shrinking pool. Within it we saw a leech, flaying about in the warming water. We decided to rescue it, gathering it up in our water bottle along with some waterweed. When we walked back to the car, we transferred it into an empty jam jar, where it groped about blindly throughout the rest of our trip.

Our journey ended at a campsite somewhere along the Coorong. Mother found an especially remote park, practically deserted despite it being high tourist season. We set up our tent just up from the beach, looking out over the ocean, and bought a large bag of hot potato chips for dinner.

Late in the night, a thunder storm rolled in. It struck with such unrelenting force it seemed like we were being attacked. One by one, it ripped the tent pegs out of the earth, and the canvas collapsed down upon us. I cowered beneath it, listening to the boom of the thunder. I was certain we would soon be blasted into oblivion, or drowned. Mother, undeterred, scrambled out to assess the damage.

When, after several terrifying minutes, she had not returned, I stuck my head out of the tent to look for her. The rain was blinding. 'Mother!' I cried, 'Mother!'

She appeared through the downpour, hammering the ten pegs back into place. When she secured the last one, she pulled the ropes taut and the tent suddenly rose around me. She raised her arms in triumph and emitted a roar of victory. As she did so, a sheet of lightening spread across the sky, illuminating her plump silhouette. The air crackled with a final shudder of thunder and the rain suddenly stopped, leaving the world dark and silent. Mother climbed back into the tent, giggling.

We drove home the next day, following a scenic backroad through the hills. Late in the afternoon, she decided we should stop for a picnic, and we followed a fire track into a thickly wooded forest, entirely devoid of signage. We parked the car, and walked down a goat track until we found ourselves, inexplicably, inside a grove of ancient oak trees.

It was unlike anything I had seen before, or since, in Australia. The ground was littered with acorns. After we finished our picnic, we gathered up a handful as a memento and, when we got home, scattered them outside the living room window. Within weeks, three saplings appeared, entwined and growing at an uncanny rate.

It was a wonderful holiday. I think she enjoyed it as much as I did. In her diary, she wrote:

> I like the conversation in the car with the complicated questions that I have the time and freedom to answer. 'Why are ants so small?' 'Where did the dinosaurs come from?' 'Do you want a penis?' 'Why can't I have a baby?' or the more difficult ones, 'Will there be a world when we are both dead?'

Together, we mended some of the fraught nerves of the previous year. I was, she thought, observant, interesting, and inquisitive. I no longer seemed scared, and had hardly cried at all. She thought the holiday had done me good.

When I think of my mother now, I think of her as she was then: thirty-three and still strong and young, despite the effects of Cushing's Syndrome. I think of her as she looked when I sat next to her in the car; in profile, looking ahead, answering my questions without taking her eyes off the road.

15

> Of all the art forms, poetry is the most economical. It is the one which is the most secret, which requires the least physical labor, the least material, and the one which can be done between shifts… A room of one's own may be necessary for writing prose, but so are reams of paper, a typewriter, and plenty of time.
> — Audre Lorde

In the week before school resumed, Mother built a small pond in the front yard, into which we placed the leech, two goldfish, and a water lily. On the first day back in class, the teacher asked each student to report on their summer holiday. I duly announced I had a pet leech. She thought I was lying and rang up my mother, who assured her I was telling the truth.

I had an easier time of it after that. I think I became an accepted oddity among my classmates. One afternoon I decided to pretend I was a dog, and spent my lunch break crawling about the playground holding a stick in my mouth. No one laughed at me or made any harsh comments. I was, more or less, left to my own devices.

I still disliked going to school, but I grew resigned to it. Each morning I would approach the classroom with the attitude of someone who suffers from bad dreams. I accepted seven hours of each day would be unavoidably unpleasant, but that these hours were nothing more than a mirage. When the final school bell rang, I would wake up, dash home to Tubby, and return to the impenetrable safety of the garden.

By contrast, Mother's life was growing more difficult. She had been working at the same school for two years, but remained closeted at work. It irked her. She decided to come out to one of her colleagues, a woman of her own age, whom she felt she could trust. The response was not encouraging; the woman turned away and pretended to be sick. Later, she apologised, but Mother was upset.

After that, she became less sociable. I remember her talking to friends on the phone but I was no longer forced into playdates, and she stopped inviting people over. She did not seek out another romance. On weekends we visited my grandparents, or my aunt, or joined my grandmother in trailing through school fetes and garden stores, but mostly we kept to ourselves.

The neighbourhood certainly didn't grow more welcoming with time.

Early in my second year at school, we had found a stray kitten wandering around the river. We took him home, and I called him Boris. He had a sweeter temper than Ginger, although the two got on well. They spent their time gambolling about the back garden, or curling up together in sunny spots in the nasturtiums. One afternoon we found him dead. He had, Mother thought, been poisoned. We buried him beneath the mandarin tree.

Not long after, Ginger limped in with a broken leg. Our vet said someone in the neighbourhood had taken to killing cats. They had been setting up traps throughout the neighbourhood.

'That's probably what broke his leg,' he told us. 'They've also been throwing lumps of poisoned meat into people's yards. You should keep an eye out.'

We didn't find any, but later Ginger was poisoned. We rushed him to the vet but he died as well, so we buried him next to Boris.

Those final years of the twentieth century have a retrospective aura of dull complacency, trailing after the tumult of the sixties and seventies, and overshadowed by the ill-fated wars and economic upheaval of the twenty-first century. I suppose things were happening: the Falklands War, US incursions into South America, the fall of the Berlin Wall, and so on. Yet when I think of that time, I remember it through this sequence of strange events: mother's friend retching in the staff room, Ginger shivering as he died, and tiny Boris, laying stiff in the grass. They were at once intimate yet impersonal, banal yet full of menace.

Of the greater, global events, the only one I can really remember is the Black Monday market crash in October 1987. I was finishing Grade Two, and just a few months short of my eighth birthday. I mostly remember it because it was something Mother couldn't explain. 'It's a recession,' she told me, 'which means people are going to lose their jobs and have less money. I'm not really sure why.'

I was surprised. I assumed she knew the answer to everything, or at least had an opinion about it. In fairness, it was a difficult question. Unlike earlier downturns, the 1987 crash lacked any discernible cause, such as a credit crunch or an oil crisis. Share trading had just been computerised but the trading algorithms were imperfect, leading to a spiral of sell orders that wiped out most of the major indices. The Australian market dropped by 40%. As a result, the entire state of South

Australia went bankrupt, entering into a period of economic malaise from which it never fully recovered.

When the state election rolled around, the Liberal opposition put up billboards listing how much every South Australian owed. 'Why do we owe money?' I asked my mother.

'Because the state bank collapsed, and now the government is broke.'

'Who do we owe money to?'

'Lots of people, I think.'

A few weeks later, at the start of the Christmas holidays, we were driving to the shops when we noticed large posters stuck to all the telephone poles and fences. One warned the government had been taken over by 'Poofs and Wogs.' Another foretold an impending 'Yellow Peril.' A third was emblazoned with the slogan, 'Bomb Them!' and, below that, a picture of a boat.

'What does it mean?' I asked my mother.

'It's a picture of a refugee boat.'

'But what does it mean?'

'The people who put up the posters don't like refugees coming to Australia in boats, so they think they should be bombed.'

'But who would bomb them?'

'I think they want the government to bomb them.'

'But why?'

'They think the refugees caused the recession.'

Our neighbourhood was home to a chapter of National Action, akin to the British National Front, albeit with lesser organisational skills.

'Did the refugees cause the recession?'

'No.'

'So why do they want to bomb the boats?'

'When people are confused or scared, they often get angry, and then sometimes they do mean things.'

'Like bomb people's boats?' 'Yes, exactly.'

'Or poison Ginger and Boris?'

'That's probably true,' she said, and paused. I could see her thinking it over. 'That doesn't make it right, but you have to try to understand why people do things, even when they don't make much sense.'

When school started again the next year, early in the first term each child in my class was issued with a silver coin, about the same size and shape as a standard twenty cent piece, but none of us could understand why. 'It's a commemorative coin,' explained our teacher, 'To commemorate the bicentenary of the First Fleet landing in Sydney Cove.'

'How much is it worth?' asked one of my classmates. He, and several other students, wanted to use their commemorative coins to buy lollies from the school cafeteria during recess.

'They're not actually legal tender,' explained the teacher.

There was a long silence while we each thought about this. 'So you mean we can't buy lollies with them?'

'No. They're not real coins. They're just commemorative.'

The class fell silent. 'So you mean they're worthless?'

'No, they're very valuable. They're commemorative.'

Each of us stared at our coins, trying to figure out what they meant.

The next week, we were all given 'settler' costumes and taught to march in formation around the basketball court, singing the first verse of the national anthem over and over again. The settler costumes consisted of flannel shirts and neckerchiefs for the boys, and pinafores for the girls.

'Why do we have to wear these costumes?' asked one of my classmates.

'Because the people on the First Fleet wore them when they arrived in Sydney.'

'Did the settlers use commemorative coins?'

'No, of course not.'

The following week the principal announced we would all be made to attend a new class on Australian history. Instead of our regular teacher, it was taught by Mr Porter, who usually taught the senior grades. Every Tuesday morning for the following term, he would stride into our class room brandishing a series of video tapes containing a multipart television series based on AB Facey's *A Fortunate Life*. After each episode, he would talk about the Australian landing at Gallipoli before segueing into an account of his own father's time in the air force during the Second World War.

He was, I suppose, not trained as a historian but what he lacked in technique he made up for in emotion. After we finished the video tapes, most of his lessons consisted of heartfelt speeches on the sacrifice of Australian soldiers abroad. The context for their sacrifice remained unclear.

'Where is Gallipoli?' one of my classmates asked.

'It's in Turkey,' Mr Porter told us.

'Why were there Australians in Turkey?'

'There weren't. They were trying to land on the beaches.'

'So they were trying to invade Turkey?' asked a particularly astute boy, of Italian heritage.

Mr Porter abruptly flipped over his desk and bellowed, 'If the Japs had invaded Australia, you wouldn't be here today!'

There was a shocked silence. The desk was put back in place, and Mr Porter continued his soliloquy on Gallipoli. At lunch, we all gathered together, trying to make sense of it.

'Were the Japanese in Turkey?' asked one of the girls.

'No, I think the Japanese were in the Second World War. Gallipoli was in the First World War,' someone else suggested.

'How many world wars have there been?'

None of us could figure it out. I asked my mother, who confirmed there had been two world wars, only one of which involved Japan. 'So why did Mr Porter get so upset about the Japanese?' I asked her.

'Because Mr Porter is an idiot. There's a new curriculum module,' she explained, 'All public schools are being sent an Australian history colouring book full of pictures of the First Fleet. All the senior teachers want us to adopt it. It's not even historically accurate. The pictures are mostly just stock images of pirate ships.'

Aside from her frustrations at work, she had other, more material concerns. As a result of the recession, the interest rate on her mortgage had gone up again, and the repayments were proving insurmountable. She decided she needed a better job, one with a bigger pay cheque, and more control over the school curriculum.

She enrolled in night classes for a Post-Graduate Diploma in Education from the University of South Australia, hoping to make her way into management. 'I'm going to classes until late every Wednesday night,' she explained to me, 'Your grandmother is going to take care of you. You'll need to be a good boy.'

I was entirely unsupportive. On the nights of her tutorials,

I would accuse her of abandoning me, burst into tears, and beg her not to go. On top of that, Gran was an unenthusiastic babysitter. She disliked having to drive down from the hills every week, and found my melodrama galling. After I finished crying, I usually spent the evening watching television and playing with Tubby. She found this painfully dull, so she would drag me off for a brisk march along the river. I would trail after her complaining.

At that time, Gran was particularly ferocious. She had just turned sixty, an experience she described as akin to becoming partially invisible. People began referring to her as 'dear' and she found herself patiently and politely ignored. She responded by wearing extremely bright clothing, which she made herself using an array of fluorescent and metallic fabrics. The effect was so striking that, on sunny days, she became quite literally blinding.

For her sixty-first birthday, we bought her a metallic blue baseball cap with a glittering sticker of a butterfly upon the peak. She wore this for the following decade, making outfits to suit. It made her easy to find in crowds, although it did not improve her mood.

Gran stopped babysitting after an incident with the flame tree in our front yard. It had sprouted a branch, extending out over the front path, at the exact height of her forehead. Inevitably Gran walked into it. Furious and blinded by pain, she grabbed a pair of secateurs and hacked at the branch until it fell away. When Mother arrived home from her night classes she was outraged.

After that, my mother hired a babysitter, although this produced its own complications. One night shortly before her graduation, the babysitter turned up trailing a huge mixed-breed dog, which she had found wandering alone, apparently abandoned. After some debate, it was decided he was a combination of Rhodesian Ridgeback, German Shepard, and several less definite breeds. He had probably been dumped on account of his colossal size.

'Can we keep him?' I asked Mother.

'No, he's much too large for us to take care of. We'll find his owners, or we'll find someone else to take care of him.'

'But I want to keep him.'

'I'm sorry dear, but he's just too big.'

By the time she arrived home from her night class I had named him Dennis and we had become the very closest of friends. Mother spent the next week phoning the council asking if anyone had reported a lost dog. Each morning, when she went to work, she left him in the front yard with the gates open, hoping he would wander off. Yet when we returned each night he would greet us enthusiastically at the gate.

By this time, Mother's wire-haired terrier, Suzie, had gone to the great doghouse in the sky, both our cats had been poisoned, and our only pet was her aging terrier, Cassie. Despite their differences in size and age, Cassie and Dennis became inseparable. After two weeks, when she still hadn't found his owner, Mother begrudgingly decided he could stay. She had grown fond of him as well. He was an unrelentingly cheerful animal, which she appreciated.

He was not, however, without his faults. When we left the house, Dennis spent the time until our return destroying our possessions, shredding upholstery, ripping up shoes, and on his worst days, attacking the furniture. He had an extreme and cunning gluttony, routinely breaking into our cupboards and gorging himself to the point of sickness. We would arrive home to find he had not only consumed all our food but then voided it in huge mounds throughout the house. Yet he was always so happy to see us, and so contrite when scolded, that he was inevitably forgiven.

To curb his energy, Mother insisted I walk him every morning before school. Dennis found his walks overwhelmingly exciting and bolted as soon as I opened the front gate. He was far stronger than I, and inevitably eluded my grip on his lead, whereupon Mother and I would spend the next half hour chasing him through the neighbourhood. She would arrive late to work, frazzled, sweating, and easy fodder for the petty sniping of her workmates. On the upside, with Dennis for company I became less demanding and she was able to continue her night classes in relative peace.

In those days, it was still common for vocational education to involve some glimpse of higher purpose, so she took an elective in the Department of Women's Studies called 'Autobiography and Creative Writing.' It gave her a few hours of intellectual conversation with people to whom she could speak openly, an experience she had been denied for some years.

As part of the class, she studied *A Room of One's Own,* with its oft cited mantra that 'it is necessary to have five hundred a year and a room with a lock on the door if you are to write fiction or poetry.' Inspired, she submitted one of her own poems for inclusion in the course's end-of-year magazine:

> Have you ever shared a bed
> With two dogs and a boy?
> It's rather cramped.

You don't sleep well.
A bed of one's own and $30,000 a year.

After she graduated, she showed me the magazine, with her name listed in the contents page. I was immensely impressed.

With her new qualifications, she applied for a job at another school: teaching the Grade Sevens and advising on curriculum development. It was located in a suburb otherwise known for its motorcycle gangs, militant racists, drug dealers, and large population of new migrants who couldn't afford to live anywhere else. One of her students, aged twelve, missed several weeks of class because she injected her brother, aged seven, with heroin. Another used his Monday morning show-and-tell session to talk about helping his parents steal their neighbour's marijuana crop. A third was suspended only to return wielding a knife and demanding revenge.

Confronted with such challenges, Mother flourished. The petty bigotries of her previous workmates were replaced by a collegiality forged in constant crisis. Instead of arguments over the merits of colouring-in, she spent her staff meetings discussing the best methodologies for teaching mathematics and improving literacy.

She came out at work for the first time. In her diaries she wrote, 'I am not closeted at work to co-workers and a select safe group of parents. I feel just about proud.' After a few months, she was promoted and, the following year, asked to fill in as Acting Deputy when the usual incumbent went on leave.

By the time of her promotion, it had been fifteen years since her kidney transplant. She was entering her late thirties, and her doctors conceded she was likely to live through her forties, and possibly even make it into old age. She formed a habit of loudly announcing, 'I will live until I'm eighty!'

16

> As we approached the Shore they all made off, except two men who seem'd resolved to oppose our landing [...] We then threw them some nails, beads, etc... which they took up, and seem'd not ill pleased with. [A]s soon as we put the boat in again they came to oppose us, upon which I fir'd a musquet between the two, which had no other Effect than to make them retire back...and one of them took up a stone and threw at us. — Captain Cook, April 29, 1780.

Our finances improved after Mother started her new job, although she now left the house at quarter to eight in the morning, and didn't return until six in the evening. We still had breakfast together every morning, and she dropped me at school each day, but I walked home alone, and spent three or four hours by myself until she returned. At night, she was usually too tired to cook, so we had sandwiches for dinner, or sometimes got a takeaway.

In the middle of the year, I started getting stomach aches, accompanied by prolific flatulence. After our evening sandwiches, I would spend an hour or two huddled on the toilet emitting acrid fluids. The next morning the same thing would happen again, after I had my Weet-bix, and Mother would ring my school and tell them I was too sick to come to class.

Our doctor thought I was allergic to milk and wheat. Both

were such staples of the suburban diet it seemed unthinkable anyone could be allergic to them. Accordingly, it took him three months to reach a diagnosis. During that time, I was sick at least one or two days each week. As Mother needed to work, and Gran had not been forgiven for the incident with the flame tree, I was left home alone.

'If anything goes wrong, or you hurt yourself, phone the receptionist at my school and ask for me,' Mother told me when she left.

'What if I can't get through? Should I phone Gran?'

'Only if you absolutely have to. I don't want her coming down here and cutting down any more trees.'

I was very happy with the situation. After an hour or two on the toilet, I usually felt fine, and spent the rest of the day playing in the garden, before settling down in front of the television to watch my favourite shows.

By then, the garden was so dense that parts of it had become inaccessible. Sometimes Mormons or door-to-door sales people would try to make it to our front door only to become ensnared in nasturtium tendrils and forced to retreat. The postman complained he was regularly struck by branches as he tried to deliver our mail. Our neighbours hated it.

One of them, a wizened old man on the southern border, made a point of standing on the fence line cursing loudly. Each morning, we would hear him cutting back foliage that had crossed over into his property, and hurling it back into our yard.

Mother liked to stand outside, listening to him and giggling. 'His problem is he thinks that a love of order equates to a love of gardening, but he's wrong.'

She had a point. His house was uniform, bordered by a

grim but neatly clipped lawn, which varied in colour, from a faded khaki in the winter months to a light brown in summer. He spent hours tending to it, but it looked terrible and made him miserable. Every Saturday we could hear him yelling at his lawnmower as he dragged it across the lifeless turf.

In the early summer, Mother prepared a flower bed along the fence line in the front garden, into which she mixed several bags of cow manure and a soil additive called 'Blood and Bone'. The name was literal; it consisted of a nitrous substance scraped from the floors of abattoirs. Into this concoction she planted an especially thorny climbing rose.

When the February heatwaves arrived, the soil smelt so bad it made my eyes water, but the rose bush flourished. When Mother got home from work each day, she checked its progress, watching as it extended both blooms and thorns upwards, over the neighbour's fence, and across the path that led to his letter box. Each morning, as he collected his mail, we would hear him coughing amid the odour of fertiliser, cursing as he stumbled headlong into the rose bush, and then crying in pain as the thorns gored his bald scalp.

He complained to my mother, but she merely smiled and assured him he could trim it back if he wanted. They both knew this was impossible. Pruning only spurred it on. One day Mother arrived home from work to discover the rose bush withered and reeking of lawnmower fuel.

That night, I ate a packet of chocolate biscuits and, as a result, had to stay home from school the following day. I spent the morning building a fort in the backyard, and then came indoors to take a nap. I was awoken by the sound of our front gate opening. As I peeked from behind the living room curtains,

I saw our neighbour sneak into our yard and shuffle over to inspect the rose bush. For several minutes, he contemplated its blackened leaves, nodded his head contentedly, and shuffled away.

I phoned Mother's school but she was out on a field trip. Then I phoned my grandmother. Twenty minutes later, I saw her car pull up and heard the door slam. The foliage obscured my vision, but I could see the sun flickering off her baseball cap as she stormed into the neighbour's yard and began banging on his door. For several long moments, I could hear her yelling at him, and make out his occasional whimpers of protest.

When Mother arrived home from work, we told her the whole story. The neighbour had claimed he was trying to kill aphids, before backing down completely and offering an unreserved apology. He never bothered us again. For once, Mother could find no fault in Gran's actions. The incident with the flame tree was immediately forgotten.

A week later, my mother and grandmother decided the three of us should embark upon a driving holiday together. They thought it would be good for me to see the country. Mother took ten weeks of long service leave, I was pulled out of school for a term, and Gran told my grandfather he would be staying home with the dogs while she took their car and caravan. The three of us set off to roam the Australian countryside like Boudica and her marauding armies.

'When do you think you'll be back?' asked my grandfather.

'I think somewhere between seven and ten weeks but I can't be sure,' Gran told him. He looked concerned.

On the first morning, as we waited to pull out of the driveway, he fidgeted about, nervously checking the caravan's tyres and topping up the car's radiator fluid. 'Where do you think you'll stop tonight?'

'Oh, I don't know. Somewhere along the river I expect.'

'Don't forget the handbrake on the caravan. You have to turn it on when you park each night, and then turn it off when you leave in the morning.'

'Stop fussing. I know how to handle a caravan.'

We drove to Renmark, where we found a small museum, staffed by an extremely old man. He was very excited to see us. 'I like your hat,' he told my grandmother. 'Would you like a ticket for the museum? It's got some very interesting antique farm machinery.'

'Is there a caravan park near here?'

'Yes, there is. I can write down directions for you if you'd like. Did you know the cask wine box was invented here in Renmark? Are you sure you don't want tickets to the museum? It really is a very good museum.'

My grandmother frowned at him, but we still bought tickets to the museum. It consisted of several sheds full of rusted farm equipment. Afterwards, we followed the man's directions to the caravan park. Next morning, we were driving down the highway when we noticed smoke coming from the wheels of the caravan. We had forgotten to turn off the handbrake. The brake pads had been destroyed.

'Do we need them?' asked my mother.

'Probably not.'

We drove on. Each night, we stopped in a different town and visited whatever local attractions it had to offer. Each morning Mother and Gran would sit at the breakfast table in the caravan, consulting a large road map, and debate our next destination.

Slowly, we wove inland, seeking out regional botanic gardens, seasonal fetes, and unusual geological or historical landmarks.

In the mid-eighties, regional Australia still had its own eclectic tourism industry. The riverside town of Mildura had a garden maze, Echuca hosted a surprisingly good wax museum, and Dubbo had a zoo with a small island housing all the monkeys who had escaped from zoos elsewhere in the country. In Coonabarabran there was a theme park called Miniland, paradoxically full of life- size fibreglass dinosaurs. I was fortunate to be one of the last generations of children to enjoy these spectacles. A spike in insurance premiums shut most of them down a few years later, and the rest were finished off by cheap family flights to Bali.

One afternoon we stopped at a regional gallery which, by chance, was hosting an exhibition of William Morris prints. Inevitably, his famous quote was emblazoned on the wall, and printed on several tea towels in the gift shop:

> If you want a golden rule that will fit everything, this is it: Have nothing in your house that you do not know to be useful or believe to be beautiful.

My mother and grandmother stood pondering it together for some time. Both thought it was a noble sentiment.

'I think it's a lovely motto,' Mother concluded.

'Yes, so do I,' agreed my grandmother. There was a long pause. 'Do you remember you used to have that stupid magazine rack?' Gran continued.

'It was a very good magazine rack.' They fell into silence again. 'Maybe we should get Dad one of the tea towels?'

My grandmother agreed. We purchased two tea towels, ate three slices of carrot cake from the cafeteria, and sent my grandfather a postcard of Morris and Co wallpaper. I don't remember the two of them bickering at all after that. They seemed united by some wandering star only they could see. It was the first time I realised how very similar they were.

After seven weeks of wandering, we drove into Sydney, where we rented a serviced apartment on the North Shore, overlooking the harbour. It was the first time I had seen a town bigger than Adelaide and I thought it was magical. Each day, we caught the ferry over to the city, wandering along the foreshore between the museums, art galleries, and public parks. We walked through The Rocks, and looked at the ships coming in and out of Circular Quay.

'Is this where Captain Cook landed?' I asked my grandmother.

'He didn't come in to Sydney Harbour. He went into Botany Bay for a bit, but he didn't stay very long.'

'My teacher says he founded Australia.' 'A lot of people say that.'

'What did he actually do?'

'Made a nuisance of himself mostly.'

Gran was a big reader of Australian history, and had a knack for succinct summaries. We visited a number of other historic sites, where she offered descriptions vastly at odds with the things Mr Porter had told me. I had a fabulous time.

It took us another three weeks to drive home. By the time we returned, all three of us glowed with good health, washed clean of our anxieties. My allergies had disappeared. Flinders Park, however, remained the same. I had assumed my absence would put me behind in class, but I found the opposite was true. I had been absent for an entire term, but had missed nothing of academic importance.

As the year drew to a close, our teacher explained we would soon be entering the senior class, and then going on to high school. After this, he explained, we would need to get jobs. I suppose I knew this was true in theory, but hadn't really thought about it in practice.

'What happens if we don't get a job?' asked one of my classmates.

'It's not really a choice, you need to get a job.'

'So it's compulsory? A bit like school?'

'Yes, it's a lot like school, except you don't get as many holidays, and you have to stay until five.'

It struck me I might never enjoy the kind of freedom I had enjoyed on our driving holiday again. In one of our classes, we were asked to think about what we wanted to do when we grew up. I decided I wanted to become a monk, although I had the good sense not to say this out loud.

It was a strange choice for a ten-year-old boy. I'd been inspired by a book my grandmother had given me, written by Rosemary Sutcliff, that focused on the adventures of a small boy, socially ostracised due to his deformed leg. He finds solace in the isolation of a monastery, devoting himself to herb gardening and the healing arts.

I'm not sure what Mother made of it. Outwardly she was supportive. She bought me a book on Benedictine monks, made me a habit out of an old bedsheet, and helped me build a medicinal herb garden beneath the apricot tree. Here I spent many happy hours, dressed in my makeshift habit, planting medicinal plants. With my return to school, my stomach problems had resumed so I focused mostly on herbs with ostensible healing properties for the digestive system.

My pursuit of a monastic life fell apart when I had my first serious encounter with organised religion. A group of Anglican parents cajoled the school principal into allowing them to implement a Religious Education class, although the only religion we studied was Anglicanism. I didn't understand the difference between Benedictine Monks and suburban Anglicans, so I approached it with enthusiasm, thinking it might help me pursue my intended career.

I was disappointed. The Anglicans based most of their lessons on parlour games loosely associated with popular bible stories. At the end of each class, they would attempt to tie everything together with a short speech. I listened to these with an open mind, until one of the Anglicans tried to illustrate the concept of grace by comparing it to a video of Michael Jordan performing a slam dunk. Michael Jordan's slam dunks were impressive but I had expected something greater of God Almighty.

The Anglicans had given me an illustrated bible for children. I tried reading it but thought it was terrible. Was it possible to be a monk without believing in God? I thought not. I was approaching my eleventh birthday and the inevitable transition out of boyhood began that summer when, just before the start of the Christmas break, my father died unexpectedly of an aneurism.

17

> Eccentricity has always abounded when and where strength of character has abounded; and the amount of eccentricity in a society has generally been proportional to the amount of genius, mental vigour, and moral courage it contained. That so few now dare to be eccentric marks the chief danger of our time.
> — John Stuart Mill

Although I barely knew my father, I mourned his death. It would be disingenuous to say I mourned him as a human being. All up, I probably spent less than two days with him. Still, when a parent dies you lose not only the person, but an idea of parental love, or care, or a sense of where you come from. That loss is significant, no matter how you feel about the person.

I learned of my father's death on a late afternoon in December, when my mother and grandmother appeared in the doorway to my classroom, asking if I could be excused. We walked to my grandmother's car, where Mother announced, 'Your father has died,' and then burst into tears.

'What happened?' I asked.

'They found him in his car, and they thought he was asleep. But he was dead. The doctors say a blood vessel in his brain burst.'

I had last seen him three months earlier, when he took me to the Royal Adelaide Show. We invested heavily in a game where we placed ping pong balls in the rotating fibreglass head of a clown. Later, he bought me an array of novelty joke items, including a bar of soap which made your hands dirtier rather than cleaner. He explained that I could use this with comic effect on my mother. She would, he thought, find it very amusing.

Two weeks later he rang to ask if my mother had used the novelty soap yet. This was unusual as he had never called me before. Gran and my mother speculated he was on the cusp of some sort of paternal revelation, but I don't remember any other evidence of this. I do remember the phone conversation. Mother had not used the soap. Most likely she spotted it as a fake and left it undisturbed on the bathroom sink. My father told me to be patient. Timing, he explained, was the essence of comedy.

He then offered me the only piece of fatherly advice he ever gave: if you farted while in the bath, you should capture the bubbles in a face towel. This would mean whoever subsequently used the face towel would get a whiff of flatulence. As a ten-year-old, I thought this a master stroke of comic genius, although I later discovered it doesn't work. That was the last time I spoke to him.

We went to his memorial service, at a small funeral home in the city. His body was displayed in in his folk band uniform, an outfit reminiscent of the 'settler' costume I had worn at school. His wife and children were sitting in the front row, looking miserable. Mother and I sat in the third row, and I clutched her hand while she wept. We listened to the various speakers, talking about his virtues and how much he loved his family. Mother and I were not mentioned.

The two of us walked out of the tiny chapel and into the summer sunshine together. I was neither upset nor surprised that we had not been acknowledged. It struck me I had been dealt a perverse stroke of good luck. Statistically, Mother had been far more likely to die than my father. Had I been attending her funeral, I knew I would be profoundly alone and unprotected. By contrast, his death left me, materially at least, undisturbed.

Mother spent the following week crying with a velocity I had never seen before and never saw again. In her journal, she devoted several pages to digesting my father's death, writing:

> I always thought we would laugh again, share our love
> and be proud of the boy together, but you're dead at 36.
>
> The sun has shone all day, my garden is beautiful, and
> our son sings old folk songs and laughs.

In his memory, we planted a pepper tree in a spot behind the shed. We made quite a ceremony of it. This, Mother explained, would give us a place to contemplate his life and remember his legacy.

Later, she forgot this incident entirely. When I was in my thirties, she insisted we planted the pepper tree to celebrate my eleventh birthday. She told me she viewed it as a metaphor for my growth and took great joy when it became so immense the neighbours complained about it.

It was a telling lapse of memory. The nature of her ill-health meant she had prepared herself for the loss of her own life very well, but I do not think she had ever seriously contemplated the death of anyone she loved. As such, my father's death came as an immense shock. Over time, I think she came to see it as an anomaly, brought about by his taste for cigarettes and fatty food.

I think she saw mortality as something over which she held a privileged monopoly. She was, in her way, correct. My father was the only person she loved who had the audacity to die before her. When my grandparents grew into their eighties and began to show the inevitable markers of old age, she treated their various illnesses like personal faults.

Whenever my grandmother had any sort of health problem, Mother would call me to complain. 'Your grandmother is in hospital again. It's her own fault. She doesn't drink enough water. I've told her she needs to stay better hydrated, but she doesn't listen to me.'

After each episode, I would suggest she could be kinder. Gran, I explained, was not responsible for the ravages of old age, and would not live forever, no matter how much water she drank. Mother would accept my argument in principle, but reject it in practice. I don't think she ever fully grasped the idea her parents were mortal.

In this respect, the death of my father was the first point at which I felt a glimmer of distance between Mother and I. She saw mortality as something she could fend off with sheer, brutish will power, just as she had survived her kidney transplant. I saw it as a chaotic existential threat which might remorselessly kill one's loved ones without the faintest warning.

In the summer after my father's funeral I fell to contemplating the impending death of the people I loved: my mother, my grandparents, my aunts and uncles, my pets and even, eventually, myself. There was, I concluded, nothing I could do about it. Briefly, I revisited my monkish aspirations, as the Anglicans had said faith was a great comfort in times of sorrow. When that failed, I developed an obsessive anxiety, fretting constantly that Mother was going to die.

She inadvertently provided fodder to my phobia. In the year after my father's death, she was hospitalised twice. Neither incident was life threatening, but I found them terrifying nonetheless. The first occurred when she was moving bales of hay between the front and back garden. One of the bales contained a venomous spider, which bit her on the upper thigh. She was not wearing trousers at the time, as she often liked to do her Saturday morning gardening in her underpants. The lack of a protective layer allowed the spider to inflict substantial damage.

Mother had been bitten by spiders before and saw them mostly as a minor annoyance. Unfortunately, this one had been especially noxious and the bite mark blossomed into a bulbous patch of rotting skin. She ignored it for several days until begrudgingly reporting it to her doctor, who immediately sent her into day surgery where they gouged out a large chunk of flesh from her upper leg.

Some complication associated with her transplanted kidney made it unsafe for her to receive a local anaesthetic, so she underwent the operation with nothing more than three household painkillers and a foam stress ball. I sat in the waiting room outside, fidgeting with nerves. Eventually she emerged, limping slightly but unperturbed. When we got home, she showed me the bandage covering the wound and explained I had no need to be afraid.

The second incident occurred in winter, when she developed an inexplicable enthusiasm for sewing. Her enthusiasm was matched by an equally lackadaisical attitude towards pins and needles, a number of which ended up on the floor and gradually worked their way into the matted and muddy carpet. Inevitably she trod on one, whereupon it broke in half, leaving a two-centimetre metal splinter lodged deep in her foot.

She refused to accept this had happened and walked about with the broken needle in her heel for four days. Eventually she went to the doctor, who sent her to have it x-rayed. The resulting surgery required her to stay in hospital overnight, and I was left in my grandmother's care. I spent the time mooning about like a Dickensian waif. Gran found it very annoying. Mother was discharged, and came home with the needle fragment in a plastic jar, which we placed on the mantelpiece above our electric heater.

Mother viewed both incidents as comical rather than life-threatening. Neither left much of an impact. She got bored of sewing shortly afterwards, although we continued to find pins scattered through the house for years. For two months she wore trousers while doing her morning gardening but, when the weather grew warmer, she reverted back to her underpants.

I began to have a recurring dream, in which we were driving to my grandparent's house for lunch and passed the wreck of our own car on the side of the road. When we arrived, I discovered Mother had disappeared. Gran told me she had died in a car crash. For several minutes, I wandered from room to room, grappling with the shock of Mother's death. Even after I woke up, the vision remained as painful as the actual death of my father.

Over the course of the following year, I became obsessed with the idea that my dream was a premonition. I insisted on travelling with her whenever possible as I thought it better that we die together. If she arrived home from work more than fifteen minutes late I would inevitably be waiting by the driveway in tears.

She was not especially sympathetic. 'I don't intend to die,' she told me, 'I intend to live until I'm eighty.'

'But it doesn't matter what you intend. You could still die anyway.'

She frowned at me. 'When I was your age, they told me I was going to die of kidney failure, and I said I intended to go on living, and here I am. When I was pregnant with you, they told me I would die if I had a child. And I said, maybe so, but I intend to have a child, and here you are. Now I'm telling you, I intend to live until I'm eighty.'

I wanted very much for her to be right, but it didn't seem like dying was something you chose. I couldn't imagine my father intended to die at the age of thirty-six. He had died so quickly I doubted he even had time to think about it. Through the autumn and winter, I grew more and more anxious.

In the final, rainy weeks of August, my school organised the annual camping trip for the senior classes. I had been on the junior camps before. They usually consisted of three days of unmitigated misery. I hated them, but attended anyway because Mother thought they were good for me.

Every year we had the same conversation. 'I'm not going to make you go,' she would explain, 'but I'll be very disappointed if you don't go. I think it's a very good opportunity for you to face your fears.'

Every year, I signed up for camp, and every year, on the day of departure, I nervously vomited up my breakfast and boarded the school bus with as much stoicism as I could muster. I wanted Mother to be proud of me but I always had a horrible time. For financial reasons, the school conducted its camps during the middle of winter, booking budget hostels when they were unable to attract any other customers. My classmates and I would be bussed out with a handful of junior teachers, and then bussed home again three days later: frozen, damp, and demoralised.

The senior camp extended this experience to a full week. Mother and I had our usual conversation about it. 'You don't have to go,' Mother told me, 'but I think it would be very good for you. And I'll be disappointed if you don't.'

'But what if you die while I'm away?'

'Why are you so worried about me dying?'

'Because I'll miss you.'

'So you're afraid of missing me?'

'And I don't know how I'll be able to cope on my own.'

'I'm not going to die for a very long time, and by then you'll be able to cope on your own. And I think camp is a very good way to practice your independence. You don't need to be around me all the time to be happy.'

I begrudgingly agreed and, on the morning of my departure, stoically threw up my breakfast and boarded the school bus. The trip was even more unpleasant than usual. My allergies confounded the kitchen staff and I subsisted on semi-cooked potatoes, corn flakes, and cheap soy milk. The showers stopped working, and all of the boys in my class were obliged to queue for the use of a portable cubicle.

At my first attempt to use this device, I became confused by the hot water tap and scalded myself, creating such a disturbance it formed the bulk of my school report card. On my second attempt, my classmates decided they would try to push the cubicle over. I think this was intended more as a test of its footings than an attack on me personally, but I avoided showering for the remainder of the camp.

During the mornings, my classmates and I were forced to take part in a series of competitive sporting activities. I was terrible at all of them, provoking the scorn of my unfortunate team mates. In the afternoons, we went on long hikes through the rain. Each night, I lay awake imagining Mother was dead. Gran, I thought, was probably in her car, driving up to tell me.

By the third day, I had developed a nervous tic whereby I constantly bit at my upper lip. This, combined with a diet of undercooked potatoes and cheap soy milk, produced a large and crusted rash across my upper lip. The only mirror was in the terrifying portable shower cubicle, so I was unaware how bad the rash had become until one of my classmates told me it looked like I had shit smeared across my face.

When we got back to school, I was pleased to see Mother had come to pick me up. I was determined to show her how brave I had been and put on my most stoic face. She looked shocked. I had returned from my week away rank, malnourished, and with a scabrous moustache.

'What happened to you?'

'I couldn't shower because the other boys tried to push over the shower cubical,' I explained.

She looked at me for several silent minutes. 'You don't need to go on any more camps if you don't want to,' she said.

Afterwards, she consulted my grandmother. 'I thought camp might help him snap out of it, but he's worse than ever. When I go out in the garden, he follows me around, and he keeps biting his lip. He's given himself quite a rash.'

'Maybe camp was a bit too much,' Gran suggested, 'But I do think he needs to spend a bit more time away from you, so he can get used to the idea you're not going to die. Why don't you sign him up to a club?'

'You mean a sporting club? I don't think that would work. He's very bad at sports.'

'What about Boy Scouts? They teach a lot of skills. He might like that?' For a few brief but disastrous weeks, I attended the local chapter of the Scouts but left after I cried in one of the meetings. One of Mother's colleagues suggested karate, because they thought it helped build confidence. I went to one lesson, refused to take part in any of the exercises, and spent the time sitting in a corner by myself. After that, she enrolled me in a painting class, but all the other participants were elderly women, which I think undermined her intended outcome.

'Maybe he should spend some time with his grandfather?' my grandmother suggested.

'Do you think Dad would do it?'

'Well he's retired now, and I think he's a bit bored. I'll tell him Ianto needs a male role model.'

'Do you think he does need a male role model?'

My grandmother contemplated the question. 'Deane is a good role model, and he's male. It can't hurt.'

'Ask him if he'd take Ianto on Friday nights. Then we can go to that dance class at the community college.'

Accordingly, every Friday night, while Mother and Gran

went to their dance class, I was left alone with my grandfather. Our appointments started at six in the evening and usually went until ten or eleven at night. We began in his workshop with a lecture on a topic of his choice, followed by a light dinner, and a chess game which I almost always won. He was not the kind of man given to letting children beat him and I think he found that part of the evening quite frustrating. At the pinnacle, my record stood at fourteen wins in a row.

The earlier part of the evening, however, belonged entirely to him. In retirement, he had devoted himself to the studies he had been unable to pursue in his youth, ranging across geology, chemistry, electronics, industrial history, the fine arts, and palaeontology. For hours on end, we stood about in his workshop while he explained these to me with all the gravitas of an Oxford dean.

His knowledge was remarkably deep and detailed. He had a habit of taking multiple bodies of knowledge and rubbing them together until they revealed some unforeseen truth. I remember one particular soliloquy on the production of bronze which lasted close to three hours. Over the first hour, he described how certain types of ore were mined, crushed, and then exposed to some sort of chemical process to extract zinc and copper. He spent the second two hours focused on the smelting processes required to produce bronze itself. I could do little more than nod politely.

Writing about the art critic John Ruskin, Virginia Woolf describes perfectly the type of noble amateur intellectual my grandfather personified:

> In the restless play of his mind upon one subject after another, there is something, we scarcely know how to define it, of the cultivated amateur, full of fire and generosity and brilliance, who would give all he possesses of wealth and brilliance, but who is fated to remain forever an outsider.

He had spent his whole life working in a factory, with his formidable intellect constrained and frustrated. In retirement, all of that suppressed energy unfurled. I was the primary beneficiary of his fire, generosity and brilliance, although I didn't understand most of it.

Like Ruskin, my grandfather spent a lot of time talking about rocks, and making watercolour studies of minerals, feathers and, in prolific volumes, gum leaves. He read deeply on geology and botany but he also thought them profoundly beautiful. He liked painting them because it was an opportunity to contemplate their aesthetic virtues at length. We often discussed this, or at least he discussed it while I listened.

I suppose he did become something of a male role model, and I did grow calmer after our time together. As I grew older, I adopted a number of his traits: an interest in interdisciplinary learning, a tendency to over-explain, and an enthusiasm for deeply technical detail. These are, I think, all positive.

The stereotype of working-class men is essentially one of stupidity and coarseness, presented either as a 'salt of the earth' quality or a stupid brutishness. My grandfather was devoid of all of these traits, and I often thought of him as I entered my teens and felt the first real pressures of manhood. In that respect, he did become my role model.

That said, he did not teach me how to relate to other men. Looking back, I can see he possessed a quality in common with my mother, my grandmother and, indeed, my wider family in that he was undeniably and profoundly eccentric. This became obvious when I started high school in the following year.

18

You must either make a tool of the creature, or a man of him. You cannot make both — John Ruskin

Compared to primary school, my high school campus seemed enormous. It consisted of a shanty town of pre-fabricated, weatherboard classrooms, centred around a huge cream brick basilica, built in the Brutalist style. It had about a thousand students, aged twelve to seventeen. I remember standing in the main quadrangle on my first morning, feeling as if I had entered some vast and unruly medieval town.

It didn't take me long to fall foul of my new classmates. The school oval was surrounded by a ring of eucalypts and, one windy afternoon, their leaves were scattered across the playing fields. At the time, my grandfather was going through a phase of painting native flora and so, after the final class, I wandered around the oval, collecting gum leaves for him.

To my surprise, I was confronted by one of my classmates. 'Nice gum leaves, fag!' he yelled.

'I'm collecting them for my grandfather,' I explained.

He took this as a provocation and became extremely hostile. He must have talked about it with my classmates as, a few weeks later, two of them came up to me in the recess break to tell me their friend wanted to bash me.

'But why does he want to bash me?' I asked.

'Because he thinks you're a faggot,' they explained.

I did not understand.

'He says you're a faggot, and he wants to kick your head in.'

I doubt a week went by between the ages of thirteen and seventeen without someone expressing a desire to pummel me, although only once was I actually attacked. One afternoon towards the end of my first term at high school, I was walking across the bridge at the top of my street when I was set upon by two drunken year nines. They lifted me off the ground, held me against the railing, and threatened to throw me into the water several metres below.

'You're going in the fucking river unless you give us all your money.' one of them said.

'Yeah fag! Give us all your money. Or you're going over the edge.'

'I only have five dollars! I can give it to you if you put me down!'

They put me down, and I began rummaging in my bag for the five-dollar note Mother had given me in case of emergencies. When I found it, they both took pity on me and told me to put it back in my bag.

'You keep it. You're all right. You're all right. Look at this! Look at what we've got!'

They showed me a two-litre plastic coke bottle, half full of clear liquid. They both took elaborate swigs from it.

'We're fucking pissed! It's vodka! We're fucking pissed!'

I nodded, they both laughed, and took two more elaborate swigs. I realised they were drunk. They dragged me off the bridge, and over to a park bench next to a playground, just outside the school gate. Here, we found a third boy, laying on the ground, sobbing. I recognised him as one of the year tens, nicknamed 'Chunks.' He was heavily overweight, with pale skin and bright red hair.

'Chunks is fucking wasted.'

'Fucking Chunks! Get up you faggot!'

Suddenly, and without any apparent provocation, they began kicking Chunks, in the stomach, the ribs, and the face. He was too drunk to resist, and lay there, begging them to stop. Eventually the beating grew so severe he stopped speaking, and began to moan and gasp for breath. This sent them into an ecstasy of savagery, during which I was able to sneak away.

I was sure they would kill him, but when I got to school the next day I saw him at the morning assembly, apparently unharmed. Looking back, they were too small, and Chunks too obese, for any serious damage to have occurred.

In hindsight, most of the incidents of violence, or attempted violence, I saw at school failed to produce any result. Usually two boys would gather in the hallway, or behind the shelter shed, push each other for a bit, yell obscenities, and sometimes, exchange a couple of ineffectual blows. Yet, very rarely, something would occur to suggest the potential for real harm.

Towards the end of the second semester, a small group of boys from my year gathered in a local park with a chocolate cake and a bag of methamphetamines. I suppose they thought they were having a picnic but, after consuming the methamphetamines, one of them ate the entire chocolate cake and flew into a rage.

At some point, he picked up the cake knife and tried to stab one of the other boys. The two of them ran around the park until the second boy fled into a public toilet and locked himself in one of the cubicles. The first boy attacked the cubicle door with the cake knife until the police came and disarmed him.

The knife wielding boy was absent from school for a few weeks afterwards, but returned in the final semester. I sat next to him in computing class. He spent our lessons oscillating between exuberant good cheer and aggressively demanding my wristwatch.

At lunch time, I sat with a group of other boys who had all had similar experiences. 'I was sitting next to him in music class,' said one, 'and suddenly I felt something hot on my arm, and I turned around and he had a lighter, and was trying to set fire to my jumper.'

'He was part of my group in maths, and he told us we all had to give him our calculators or he'd bash us. We asked him why he needed them, and he said he was building a remote control that could control planes in the air.'

'He told me I had to give him my pen and I asked if I could have it back. He said he'd think about it. At the end of the class, he did give it back, but he'd taken out the little plastic tube with the ink in it.'

I suppose the teachers must have known about him, although I don't remember them ever telling him off, or keeping him away from us. When we came back to school at the start of year nine, he had disappeared and we never saw him again.

When I was growing up, the standard cultural portrait of teenage boys suggested adolescence was a series of zany masturbatory episodes, concluding when one either tricked or coerced a woman into having sex, at which point you became a man. This was the basic plot of most movies aimed at boys and young men: *Porky's*, *Revenge of the Nerds*, *Weird Science,* and, later, the *American Pie* films.

I never felt this way. At age thirteen I felt much as a goldfish might feel if it found itself unexpectedly swimming about in a pond full of pike. At the time, I assumed I was alone and that most of the boys I knew did, more or less, think and behave like their onscreen equivalents. That they did get in fights, and trick girls into sleeping with them, and spend most of their time being either crass or angry.

At university, I read Gloria Anzaldua's complaint, 'I abhor how my culture makes macho caricatures of its men' and was reminded of those years I spent at high school. It felt like something happened whereby all the boys I knew felt they had to be as cruel to each other as possible, setting ourselves up for a general distrust of other men that I still haven't resolved. Do other men feel this way? I don't really know. I've only had a few conversations about it, nearly all with gay men, and usually when very drunk. I'm sure I'm not the only man who never spoke to their school friends after graduation. When I look back at the boys I milled around with from year eight until graduation, I never thought we liked each other.

As I remember it, we were constantly trying to catch each other out. We used to talk about how rebellious we were, or how we'd given a teacher shit, or got in trouble, but we were incredibly conformist. Our favourite films were all about rugged individualists, things like *Rambo* and *Die Hard*, and yet we had strictly enforced rules about what colour backpacks we had to have, or what colour shoes, or pencil cases.

One term, I came to school with a purple backpack, rather than a blue or black one and, for the next semester, I was nicknamed 'Bag Fag', even after I begged Mother to buy me a replacement. It only stopped when another boy turned up wearing light blue shoes. We all started chanting 'Fag shoes!' at him, until three of the bigger boys picked him up and put him in a rubbish bin while the rest of us stood about watching.

Boys used to bring pornographic magazines to school, and show them to each other to prove they weren't gay. They would sit about looking at their pilfered copies of *Playboy* or *Hustler*, all swearing they did not masturbate, and that only homosexuals masturbated. It was as if we knew we had to become heterosexuals, and so we did the things we thought heterosexuals did. I'd hardly heard the word 'fag' before I went to high school and then, suddenly, it was all we could talk about. Contrary to *American Pie* and the like, we did not revel in our sexuality so much as live in fear of it.

A friend once told me he was relieved when he realised he wasn't straight. 'I was scared when I came out,' he told me, 'but I was relieved to know I wasn't like those dickheads. Being gay meant I didn't have to pretend I was stupid anymore.'

At thirteen or fourteen, I already knew I was a heterosexual, but I hadn't realised I had to act like one. It was not something my time with my grandfather had prepared me for, and it came as a shock. At fourteen, I discovered the best way to avoid mockery and physical threats was to adopt a sort of churlish, dead-eyed persona. I altered my way of speaking to use as few syllables, and as many vulgarities, as possible. This, I thought, was how heterosexual men behaved.

Mother absolutely hated it, and we began a series of regular, rolling arguments. 'You're becoming patriarchal,' she told me one day, when I was cursing about helping with the shopping, 'You need to help with the shopping. I'm your mother, not your servant.'

I knew she was right. Every time my classmates called each other faggots, I knew it was meant as an attack on homosexuality, and I knew very well my mother was a homosexual. On the other hand, I felt my patriarchal persona saved me a good deal of trouble at school.

After I graduated, I wondered what would have happened if I had been more open about Mother's sexuality. In hindsight, I doubt I would have been badly beaten up, although I would have been pushed around a lot more, and certainly bullied and teased. At the time, I thought it would be disastrous, but then everything seems more extreme when you're fourteen.

As it was, the more I aped my classmates, the safer I felt at school, and the worse my relationship with my mother became. We fought with a previously unknown intensity, causing Dennis to quiver with fear and cower behind the couch. I had little sense of what she might be feeling. It is still hard to speculate. Mother was so busy with work she had stopped keeping her diaries.

Later, I encountered an essay by the lesbian poet Audre Lorde, in which she reflected on her troubled relationship with her own adolescent son. She had, she thought, underestimated the division the spectre of manhood would place between them:

> Our sons will not grow in to women. Their way is more difficult than that of our daughters, for they must move away from us, without us. Hopefully, our sons have what they have learned from us, and a hotness to forge it into their own image.

By fifteen, I did feel I was moving away from my mother, and entering the world without her. Many of our conflicts began with a misplaced sense of abandonment on my part and, I think, a sense of betrayal on hers.

Of course, it's hardly unusual for a teenage boy to clash with his parents but, in our case, I think it held more weight as both Mother and I were surrounded by the rhetoric that a single mother, let alone a homosexual, could not successfully raise a boy. As I approached my fifteenth birthday I did start to blame her, or rather her sexuality and marital status, for my problems.

This phase probably only lasted a few months, but I felt guilty about it for years afterwards. At the time, the guilt made me feel physically ill. In the mornings, as I worked myself into my churlish persona, my stomach would begin to bloat and cramp. At first, I thought my allergies were coming back, but the stomach aches never went away, no matter how carefully I ate.

I began refusing to go to school, arguing that I was unwell. Mother accepted it for a while. At first, she was quite worried. We tried altering my diet, but it had no effect. Our doctor sent me off for blood tests but they proved inconclusive. I was then sent for an embarrassing and uncomfortable x-ray procedure to assess the healthy function of my bowel. The doctors briefly thought I might have a colonic cancer.

I viewed this with delight. 'If I have cancer I won't be able to go to school anymore.'

'Oh, for goodness sake. If you have cancer, school will be the least of your problems. You can't possibly want cancer.'

Fortunately, when the results came back the doctor announced I didn't have cancer, and then turned to me. 'So you get a stomach ache every day before school?'

'Yes, before school, and then it usually lasts most of the

morning, and sometimes into the afternoon.'

'But it starts before school?' he continued.

'Yes. It usually starts when I'm putting on my uniform each morning.'

'And do you enjoy school?'

'No, of course I don't.' The answer seemed obvious.

I think by that point, the doctor had already concluded there was nothing physically wrong with me, and the problem was nervous in origin. He had asked me similar questions several times before.

For whatever reason, on this occasion Mother suddenly began to cry. 'I just want him to have a nice time.' she sobbed.

I felt awful. She rarely cried, and I certainly never thought I could do anything to upset her so badly. She had always seemed so invincible. Begrudgingly, I promised I would begin attending classes again. It seemed I had no option.

19

> Working the soil and digging a hole are activities as primal as an embrace or coitus; it is an error to see them only as sexual symbols; a hole, slime, a gash, hardness, or wholeness as primary realities; man's interest in them is not dictated by libido; instead the libido will be influenced by the way these realities were revealed to him. — Simone de Beauvoir

At the start of year ten, my English teacher announced he was not paid enough to teach. He seemed very depressed, which was probably reasonable. Most of his students intended to drop out at the end of the year and had no interest in English. On one of our first lessons with him, a group of boys built a makeshift drum kit out of chairs and took turns playing solos. He did not try to stop them. After that, we spent his classes watching video tapes of a children's television show called *Round the Twist* while he stared forlornly out the window.

In the second semester, we were sent to a series of career advisory classes, overseen by the school counsellor. In the first session, she explained we could work in either an office or a warehouse, depending on whether we studied English and Social Studies, or Maths and Science. I was harbouring dreams of becoming an historian, or an archaeologist, or a writer, but none of these options came up.

Afterwards, I walked home, took the ladder out of the shed,

and clambered onto the roof of our house. I looked out over the neighbourhood, contemplating my future. I realised I had devoted so much time to worrying about the present I had neglected to worry about my future. If the school counsellor was any guide, it would be much the same as school, except I would be in an office or a warehouse, and I would remain there until I died. I felt very sad.

I looked down on my mother's garden, emerald and glittering. Beyond it, lay the suburbs, stretching out to the horizon, foggy with car exhaust. I imagined my adult self, wandering through that vast greyness, like the Pardoner in the *Canterbury Tales*, endlessly seeking a return to the land of my childhood:

> Thus restless I my wretched way must make
> And on the ground, which is my mother's gate,
> I knock with my staff early, aye, and late
> And cry: 'Oh dear mother, let me in!'

I don't know why I blamed my mother, although I certainly did. I'm not sure what I thought she could have done about it. Even if she'd let me stay home from school, I knew I'd have to grow up at some point.

I wasn't alone. Other boys at school had their own baffling conflicts with their mothers. Each day at school, we would recount the various injustices we had suffered at their hands. 'I asked Mum for seven dollars so I could buy a coke, a pie, and an icy pole, but she only gave me a five dollar note, so I can only get a coke and a pie, or a pie and an icy pole. What's the fucking point of that? She's fucking stupid.'

I think we knew how pathetic these arguments made us seem, but around the age of fourteen or fifteen there was a growing sense that girls and women were, in some unexplained way, responsible for our problems. I don't know where the idea came from exactly. For most of us, our mother was the only woman we knew, so they bore the brunt of it.

As we got older, though, we shifted our attention to the girls in our class. Each lunch time, one of the boys would describe some passing encounter, complaining, 'She's a fucking bitch! I asked to borrow her pen and she didn't even answer me.'

'She's a bitch!' the other boys would agree.

At that age, many of the girls were still physically bigger than us and we were, not unreasonably, frightened of them. We spoke about them frequently but, in practice, we did everything in our power to avoid them. On the few occasions a boy confessed to a crush, we would mock him until he repented.

Our society was rigidly homosocial, and women only entered it as abstract concepts. Their myth, as Simone de Beauvoir described it, was far more appealing than any reality:

> Of all myths, none is more anchored in masculine hearts than the 'feminine' mystery. It has numerous advantages. And it first allows an easy explanation for anything that is inexplicable.

We did use it to describe anything inexplicable and, as we found most things inexplicable, we used it a lot. Women and girls were the catchall explanation for why we felt bad, and what might make us feel better, for the injustices we suffered, and their potential resolutions.

After one of the final career advisory sessions, a group of us gathered outside one of the demountable classrooms to contemplate our futures. None were optimistic, but all agreed women were somehow to blame.

'If you go into a job interview,' one of the boys said, 'and there's a woman there, you won't get the job.'

This drew murmurs of confused agreement.

'It's because of affirmative action,' he clarified, 'So now all the jobs go to women.'

'Yeah,' said one of his fellows, 'Or to blacks!'

'Or to disableds!' said another.

'Or to homosexuals!'

I wonder now if they actually believed any of it. At the time, I thought they were probably wrong, but I couldn't explain why. We obviously shared a mutual pessimism about our futures, and at least they had an explanation for it.

'The boys at school say they won't be able to get jobs because of affirmative action,' I told my mother.

'That's stupid.'

'But that's how they feel.'

'People can feel whatever they bloody well want. Do you see many big companies run by black people? Do you think your life would be easier if you were in a wheelchair?'

'No, I suppose not.'

'Do you turn on the evening news and see a bunch of stories about lesbians?'

That night, I watched the evening news. I noticed it was devoted almost entirely to the doings of a very particular type of man, who seemed, paradoxically, to be doing everything, yet doing it all badly. This didn't make me feel any better.

In the third semester, the school counsellor told us to pick our courses for the senior years. We were given charts showing the kinds of office or warehouse jobs we could expect to obtain: Human Resources Officer, Security Guard, Forklift Driver, Clerical Worker.

It was, I suppose, pragmatic advice. The state unemployment rate was twelve percent. Still, at fifteen no one wants to think their future is pointless. Maybe if we'd studied political economy or history we could have made sense of it, but instead we'd been watching *Round the Twist*.

After school, I spent more and more time sitting on the roof with the Walkman Mother had given me for Christmas, listening to a cassette tape of Nirvana's *Nevermind* and feeling depressed. I thought I shared an affinity with Nirvana's melancholic frontman, Kurt Cobain because, in his suicide note, he complained he had a 'burning, nauseous stomach', just like me.

I thought I was unique in feeling depressed and isolated but later I found nearly everyone in my age group listened to Nirvana, or one of those other doleful Grunge bands. In fact, so many young people felt bad in the mid-nineties, there was a sizable industry built on angst-riddled records and films. Our local video store even had an 'Alternative' shelf, stocked with movies starring Winona Rider and Ethan Hawke, all with great soundtracks, and miserable main characters.

There was such a zeitgeist of teen angst it was being described as a generational failing; a sort of collective devolution into navel gazing. *Time* magazine published an article complaining:

> Deep down, what frustrates today's young people — and those who observe them — is their failure to create

> an original youth culture… Mini-revivals in platform shoes, ripped jeans and urban-cowboy chic all coincide with J. Crew prep, Gumby haircuts and teased-out suburban perms. What young adults have managed to come up with is either Nuevo hipster or ultra-nerd, but almost always a bland imitation of the past.

The authors, David Gross and Sophfronia Scott, concluded, 'today's young adults want to stay in their own backyard.' In my case at least, this was true, but I still think it was an oversimplification.

Ronald Reagan and Margaret Thatcher had left office by that time, but their 'no such thing as society' mantra remained. Formerly collective problems now sat squarely with the individual. Kurt Cobain cited this as an influence, telling one of his interviewers:

> The Reagan years have definitely set us back to where the average teenager feels sort of lost. There isn't much hope.

It's easy to write-off teen angst as juvenile but I don't think he was wrong. At forty, I find Nirvana unlistenable, but at fifteen, things did seem pretty hopeless.

In the final semester of the year, the English teacher resigned, taking his *Round the Twist* videos with him. There was no time to recruit someone new, so he was replaced by the school's drama teacher. She had not, I assume, taught the subject before; our lessons were thinly repackaged versions of the theatre exercises she normally taught. I thought they were sheer hell. English had always been my best subject but when I received my final report card I received a failing grade.

Mother was furious. My grades had never been brilliant, but they had always shown promise. Usually, after I brought home my report card we would count through the As and Bs, and then get a take away dinner and some sort of treat. On this occasion, I returned with a D and we had an argument.

'What do you think you're going to do if you can't even pass English?'

'It's not my fault the drama teacher is a bitch.'

'You're becoming so patriarchal. You can't blame her because you didn't do your homework. You don't even try.'

I stormed off to listen to *Nevermind*, while she stormed out into the garden to water her vegetables. I knew she was right: I was not trying, at English or anything else. Over the following afternoons, as I sat on the roof, I decided I should try to do something. I couldn't think of anything specific, but I thought something would probably come to me if I really thought about it.

A few weeks later, I saw a documentary about an artist who dug large, sculptural holes. I decided I too would pursue the art of hole digging. Instead of spending my afternoons sitting on the roof, I spent them at the very back of the yard, underneath the pepper tree, digging. I did this every day for two or three months, using Mother's garden shovel and an old pickaxe. The hole got quite deep. Each day, as I sat through my classes, I would contemplate its structure, and how I might expand upon it. When I arrived home, I resumed digging.

I think Mother initially found the hole quite alarming. As a metaphor, it certainly wasn't positive. I remember overhearing a phone call she made to my grandmother, weighing up its pros and cons. 'Yes, he says it's an art work,' she concluded, 'and it's certainly better for him to be out there digging than sitting in his room listening to his Nirvana cassette. At least he's outdoors and getting some exercise. He's been getting quite portly.'

I could hear the faint murmur of my grandmother's voice.

'No, it's beneath the pepper tree and it's so shady I can't grow anything there anyway.'

In the final semester of year ten, I spent far more time digging the hole than doing my homework. I felt better, but Mother began to view the hole with growing suspicion. At the end of the term, I received another dismal report card, with a D grade for English. I had written a highly critical review of a visiting youth theatre group and my teacher had taken a dislike to me. Mother and I had a screaming argument.

In the last week of school, I was milling about with the same group of boys who took umbrage with affirmative action. They too had received dismal grades, but it did not seem to bother them.

'You only need good grades,' said one, 'if you want to go to university.' 'University is for faggots.'

'Fucking uni students. I'm not going to uni. I'm dropping out next year.'

Year ten was the last year of compulsory school, although I had always assumed I would go on to year eleven and twelve, and then pursue a degree. I was surprised to find most of my classmates intended to drop out and seek their fortunes.

One of the boys had an uncle who was a part time manager at a golf club. The club, he told us, was offering casual positions collecting golf balls from the driving range.

'My uncle says he can get me a job collecting golf balls. He says it's a pretty good job, except you have to wear a padded suit and carry a wire shield, because they don't close the range when you're out there.'

For those willing to take the risk, he assured us, the rate of pay was a princely ten dollars an hour.

'If you're interested, I can put in a word with my uncle. They're always looking for people.'

It had not occurred to me that I could leave school at fifteen, nor had I ever contemplated a career collecting golf balls. However, if I could not even pass English, one of the few subjects I enjoyed, then perhaps the idea had merit.

That afternoon, when I arrived home, I sat in the hole and thought about it. There was, I thought, probably a greater world out there, but the portal to it was invisible to the likes of me. I looked around me, at Mother's garden. The oaks had grown taller than the house. The pepper tree, although only a few years old, loomed over the back yard like an immense blue-green storm cloud.

The more I thought about my future, the more beautiful the garden seemed to become. Within it, the seasons continued to pass, from the bright green of spring through to the elegant blues of winter. I did not want to leave, but knew I must.

Why, I thought, should I delay the inevitable? Why endure another two years of schooling? What was the difference between working in an office, or a warehouse, or on a driving range? I decided I would quit school at the end of the year to pursue a career as a professional golf ball collector. When Mother arrived home from work I announced my decision. She told me I had lost my mind.

20

> Until I was about thirty I was always planning my life on the assumption not only that any major undertaking was bound to fail, but that I could only expect to live a few years longer... But this sense of guilt and inevitable failure was balanced by something else; that is, the instinct to survive.
> — George Orwell

Mother and I spent the first week of our summer holidays yelling at each other. I told her I was going to leave school and take up a job at the golf course, she told me I was an idiot, and then we repeated ourselves. We fell into a stony silence, which lasted through to Christmas. I tried to take consolation in the hole, but I had hit bedrock and could dig no further.

When the shops opened again after Boxing Day, Mother declared we were going shopping. I followed her through the aisles of the supermarket, pushing our trolley in silence. She radiated anger. The other shoppers looked at us nervously, and scurried away. Afterwards, she declared we would visit the main branch of the council library, located in a mall several suburbs over.

'Why don't we just go to the local library?' I asked her.

'I don't want to go to the local library. We're going to the main branch.'

'But I don't want to go to the main branch. I want to go home.'

She did not respond. We drove to the main branch library, where she stormed through the shelves, with me trailing after her. After several tense minutes, she stopped abruptly at the 'O' section and gathered up all the books by George Orwell.

'You're going to read all of these before the end of the school holidays.'

I hadn't heard of George Orwell before, and didn't understand why I had to read all his books, but her rage was so immense I dared not object.

At first, I found it a depressing task. Making my way through *1984*, I recall the villain, O'Brien, announcing, 'If you want a picture of the future, imagine a boot stamping on a human face — forever.' It brought to mind the spectacle of poor, obese, redheaded Chunks being savagely pummelled by his two drunk companions.

After that, I read *Down and Out in Paris and London*, with its descriptions of browbeaten, angry men, working pointless, miserable jobs. I remember Orwell's description of them:

> They have simply been trapped by a routine which makes thought impossible.

I thought of the boys at my school. I thought of myself, resigned to a career collecting golf balls. It was a revelation. We were all, I realised, bound up in the greater tides of history. My own life bore witness to those same ideological forces: my shyness, my fearfulness, and even my flatulence could not be separated from the conditions in which I lived.

With each new Orwell text, I experienced a flurry of epiphanies. I explained each of them, at length, to my mother.

To my surprise, her responses were unexpectedly benign. 'It's all about ideology and politics. We think politics is just something politicians do, but really it's something that happens every day.'

'Yes dear,' she replied.

'But don't you see? The way we live, the way we relate to other people, everything we do is bound up in politics.'

'Yes, I know.'

I stopped digging my hole, stopped listening to my Nirvana cassette, and told her I was going back to school. I decided I would take English in year eleven and twelve, and then go to university to study literature.

A decade later, when I completed my doctorate in English Studies, I told Mother that our trip to the library was one of the formative moments of my life; the first step on my long journey into higher learning. I was very earnest about it. 'But why,' I asked her, 'Did you choose George Orwell?'

She looked confused. After some discussion, she admitted she had no recollection of the event whatsoever. 'I suppose I just wanted you to do something other than mope, watch TV, and listen to your Nirvana cassette. And also the hole beneath the pepper tree was getting quite deep and I was worried you'd hit the sewer mains.'

During my last two years at school, I adopted a new and radical spirit. I stopped speaking to my peers, and sat by myself in classes, and at lunch and recess. Inspired by Orwell's disdain for institutions, I decided I would only attend classes if I thought the teachers were actually teaching something. Otherwise, I would stay at home to pursue my own curriculum, consisting mostly of Orwell's collected essays.

At the end of the first term, my grades were up, and Mother

was very pleased, until she came home from the parent teacher interviews. 'Your social studies teacher tells me you've missed two thirds of his classes.'

'That's probably true,' I admitted.

'Why have you been skipping his classes?'

'Because he's not a very good teacher.'

'What have you been doing?'

'I have been teaching myself.'

'Your teacher thinks you're suicidal?'

'He's a fascist. I have taken charge of my own learning.'

'Are there any other classes you've been skipping?'

'I go to English, because Mr Allen is very good. But if I think I can do a better job teaching myself, then I don't see why I should waste time sitting in class.'

'Well, I suppose I should be grateful you're studying hard.'

'I am.'

'Because you need to study hard if you want to go to university.'

'I will.'

Mother spoke to my teachers, who agreed I might continue teaching myself. Most of them thought I was chronically depressed, as I had become extremely reclusive and spent my lunch breaks in the library reading the sparse collection of socialist theory.

I think Mother was proud of me, and I did quite a good job of teaching myself. I learned more in those final two years than at any other point in my schooling. Unfortunately, I focused almost exclusively on the study of British social realist fiction, which wasn't part of the matriculation examinations. At the end of year twelve, my final grades were terrible.

Mother and I had a spectacular argument about it. She accused me of not studying hard enough, and I protested it was not my fault the modern education system was stupid. We yelled at each other for a couple of hours.

'I did study hard,' I told her, 'I told you I would, and I did.'

'But you failed accounting. What if you don't get into university? What are you going to do?'

'What would I do if I'd passed accounting?'

'I'm not angry at you, I'm just worried.'

'I promise I will do my best,' I told her.

'Well. Let's wait till we see the university entrance results. You might get in after all, in which case we're arguing over nothing.'

It was a tense week. Each day, we waited to see if I would be accepted into any of the universities I had applied to. Mother decided we needed some sort of symbolically important change, to help us pass the time. 'I think we should rip up the carpets,' she told me.

After years of her indoor gardening, they were soiled beyond the point of recovery. We tried steam cleaning them once and they turned into mud. In wet weather, they felt like clay.

Together, we spent an afternoon ripping them off the floorboards, cutting them into pieces, and piling them onto the curb for hard rubbish collection. A week later, I was accepted into the Bachelor of Arts program at the University of Adelaide and, with minor exceptions, we never fought again.

And so I entered my adulthood, at least in the technical sense of the word. 'It was lovely having a baby, and you were a very sweet little boy in your way,' Mother would often say, 'but it's so much nicer having an adult son.'

I certainly found the following years easier. Although I was too shy to participate in the discussions during my tutorials or take part in the campus's social activities, I enjoyed my time at university. Having already developed a healthy taste for truancy, I skipped classes liberally and spent my undergraduate years wandering through the Adelaide CBD. By that point, the state's economic ruin had left large swathes of it deserted. I drifted between the public gardens and museums, and then started exploring the backstreets, lined with empty shops and stalled developments.

Behind a high fence off one of the main streets, I found an immense pit filled with water. From its murky depths rose two concrete obelisks, presumably the remains of an aborted office tower. Around them grew a mass of reeds, among which nested a colony of water birds. For me, these sorts of spectacles imbued humble Adelaide with the same melancholy romance Lord Byron found in the half-deserted Rome of the Eighteenth Century: 'A ruin — yet what a ruin!'

At eighteen, I also entered my first romantic relationship. It came as a shock to everyone involved. Falling in love with a woman bore no resemblance to the smutty conversations of my former classmates. My girlfriend and I talked about our university courses, and went to see bands on the weekends. We made friends with other awkward young couples. I liked having someone to talk to.

I still have no idea what the poor girl saw in me. I was still quite flatulent, covered in puppy fat, and painfully shy. A late adolescent hormonal imbalance turned my hair into a gigantic frizzy mop, which grew in scale until I appeared to be wearing a fright wig.

Mother was delighted. She saw my first romance in the same light as an artist who sees their most obtuse masterpiece critically acclaimed. She would pull my girlfriend aside, discuss my various faults and virtues, and ask for her appraisal. 'I wanted him to be sensitive,' she would explain, 'but I think that's what makes him so timid. Do you think he's shy because he's sensitive, or do you think he's just got something wrong with him? Maybe he has an anxiety disorder? Do you think that's why he's so gassy?'

My girlfriend found these talks very confusing. Sometimes they took strange and upsetting detours. Mother started trying to give her sexual advice. 'The problem with men is their hands. They're too big, so they're not useful during sex.'

The relationship petered out shortly after that, although some of the advice must have hit a nerve as that particular young lady never dated another man again.

Still, it was a confidence boost to know I was not unlovable. I felt more at ease with the world. I started talking in tutorials, and managed to secure a series of haphazard casual jobs. Indeed, it was through my first girlfriend that I got my first office job, working as a clerk in a nursing home. She had been the previous incumbent, and the role required so little skill it wasn't openly advertised. The manager simply asked around for family and friends. The only other applicants were a retiree who had never used a computer, and a fifteen-year old who cried during the interview.

True to the prediction of my school counsellor, I have been working in offices ever since. None were quite as dull as that one. Each day, I sat in a large stationery cabinet that had been converted into a small office. Here, I answered the phones, filed bits of paper, and recorded the medical details of the ageing Eastern Europeans for whom the facility catered. Our clientele were the last of that generation who survived, or in some cases participated in, Hitler's invasion of Poland. Most of them had, for better or worse, lost their minds.

Every few weeks one would die, creating a minor flurry of paperwork but otherwise my days were almost entirely the same. It was a strange place to spend the bloom of one's youth. I have an acute memory of working there on the day of the September 11 attacks. I had little actual work to do, and so I spent the day sitting in my stationery cabinet listening to the news coverage on a portable radio. It felt like something historically important had occurred, although it wasn't clear exactly what it was.

In the following weeks, it was thought terrorists were posting anthrax through the mail and I was instructed to wear a surgical face mask and rubber gloves while sorting through the nursing home's incoming correspondence. After a month, during which no anthrax was discovered, I was told this was no longer necessary.

I worked in the office at the nursing home through the rest of my degree. When I graduated, the manager offered me a full-time job, doing the same thing I was already doing. The pay was abysmal but I was told I could work my way up, ascending into the Payroll department or Corporate Governance.

'I'm not sure why they want me to work full time. Most of the time I'm just sitting about, playing with the photocopier,' I told my mother.

'I don't think you should take it,' she told me.

'But I do need a job.'

'You'll find it too dull.'

'But don't I need a job?'

'Well, we know you can get a job, so I think you should aspire for something a bit more interesting. If you want to keep studying, I don't mind helping you for a bit longer.'

I told my manager I wanted to keep working part-time, and enrolled in the English Studies Honours program. I was not a particularly good student but I worked hard. I had no plans for my future, but it did not seem to matter. I had proven I would survive, and Mother and I both began to relax.

21

> Not many words will be required now to show that Nature has no end set before it, and that all final causes are nothing but human fictions.
> — Benedict de Spinoza

As I entered my twenties, Mother entered her prime. Within our neighbourhood, most of her old foes were dead or in retirement homes. The oaks in the front yard had grown so high they gave our house an air of permanency. Our new neighbours viewed my mother with the respect afforded to immovable local characters.

When they saw us walking Dennis, they waved hello, and listened politely as Mother told them about their gardens. 'Your roses are lovely. But they need more manure. I think you should get some Blood and Bone.'

'Oh really? I'll have to pick some up from Bunnings. Thank you Dimity, and may I say your nasturtiums are looking very nice.'

Her career also reached a pinnacle. She had now been teaching for three decades, mostly in extremely difficult schools. She was well respected. Her principal offered her a job managing curriculum development. She set up new teaching plans centred on mathematics and abstract logic. Colouring-in books were banned. Her students thrived.

Her new job meant she had, for the first time, a disposable

income. She began to speak boldly about her future. 'When I retire, you can stay here and take care of the house, and I'll adopt a nomadic life, travelling around the country. Perhaps I'll even drive around the world!'

She declared she was going to buy a camper van, and we spent several weeks looking for one, second-hand. Unfortunately, the good ones were out of her price range, and the ones she could afford all had cracked engine blocks, or faulty radiators. Instead, she bought a delivery van with a tiny engine and an extremely light frame. According to the salesman, it had been owned by a surveillance company, who used it to investigate wayward spouses and workers' compensation frauds.

It had no back seats; the area behind the driver's cab was entirely open, covered by a large sponge mat to cushion the delicate technical equipment involved in spying on people. Into this space, she installed an old foam mattress, a butane gas bottle, a portable stove, and several boxes of camping equipment.

She tore the car manufacturer's logo off the front bonnet and replaced it with a rainbow flag sticker, cut into the silhouette of a cat. 'See,' she gestured, 'now it's a camper van.'

She began ringing her old friends, many of whom she had not spoken to for five or six years. 'I've got a camper van,' she told them. They invited her to join their camping trips. She joined convoys of lesbians in campers, Subaru wagons, and battered hatchbacks as they drove out into the countryside: to Daylesford, or the Coorong, or to their properties in McLaren Vale.

One of her friends gave her a large, yellow fibreglass canoe, which she hoisted onto the van's roof, claiming she would go paddling whenever she encountered a river or lake. It was so cumbersome it rarely left its perch, but it made the van easy to find in the supermarket car park.

Eventually Mother's van became so ubiquitous her friends nicknamed it 'The Van Dyke.' She thought this was very funny. They invited her to all-lesbian soup nights, craft groups, and bush walking clubs. She was very happy and started keeping a diary again, writing out lists of camping locations and snippets of poetry.

One afternoon, she came home looking sheepish. 'I've started seeing a woman,' she told me.

'That's good isn't it?'

'Yes, I think so. Probably.'

She hadn't been in love since breaking it off with Rammy, twenty years earlier. In her diary she wrote:

> Love of 46
>
> My last chance
>
> A mid-life blossom
>
> Or the beginning of a fine old age.

Her new girlfriend was also a teacher. They had a shared interest in camping and walking their dogs.

My family had a lot of conversations about it. We were happy for her, although her new girlfriend was very gloomy. She always seemed to be upset about something, and Mother was constantly consoling her. We thought it was strange, because Mother had ended all her past relationships on the grounds her partners were too cloying, or depressing, or weak-willed.

'Yes, she cries a lot,' Mother admitted, 'but she's very intelligent. I think she just needs someone to take care of her.'

'Do you want to take care of her?' I asked.

'It's not always like that. We do have a lot of fun together.'

It was true. They did have a lot of fun together. Every few weeks, they drove the Van Dyke into the countryside, stopping in isolated campgrounds or visiting small towns. Mother had no interest in pretending to be heterosexual, and she and her girlfriend made no effort to hide themselves. It made them a regular target for bigots. At one camp ground they were greeted with calls of 'Dirty dykes! We can smell you!'

At another, a group of smirking teenage boys inexplicably gave them a house key. 'I'm not sure why,' she told me, 'But I'm guessing it was a reference to something they'd seen in pornography.'

I think she enjoyed these incidents, and often boasted about them. They re-affirmed her sense that she was different; that even in middle-age she remained unconventional, independent, and openly homosexual. When she returned from her camping trips, she would tell me about her various run-ins. 'We went into this little town, parked the Van Dyke outside the fish and chip shop, and then walked down the main street holding hands. The locals looked absolutely terrified.'

Although she still wore her floral shirts, her sexuality was obvious. She was no longer closeted at work, and the Van Dyke made her very conspicuous. When she drove around the neighbourhood, with the rainbow-coloured cat sticker on the front bumper and the canoe strapped to the roof, people stopped to stare.

It was in these conditions that she entered her fifties,

outliving all previous estimates of her life expectancy by a matter of decades. She was far more cheerful, but no less wilful. She developed an aura of urgency, and seemed to be in a constant flurry of activity. She pursued her working life with ambition and zeal, launched several expansive gardening projects, and her camping trips grew ever more ambitious.

On one of them, she found a stray kitten mewing beneath a bush in the middle of nowhere. She made a bed for it in the back of the Van Dyke, fed it on long life milk and tinned meat, and then brought it home. 'I thought Dennis needed the company,' she told me.

Dennis was, by that point, quite old, but he and the kitten got on surprisingly well. He would sit nervously while she slept atop his broad back, clawing him when he tried to move. Mother was delighted. She named the kitten Dharma. 'It's a Buddhist term. It means something like 'the transcendental order of the universe.' It's a very symbolic name.'

It didn't seem particularly appropriate. Dharma was one of the most cantankerous animals I ever met. Her relationship with Dennis was sweet, but if anyone else approached her she dug her claws into them. She remained almost completely feral. Her saving grace was a complete lack of interest in the local birds, who hopped about her as she lay dozing in the garden.

'I'm not sure Dharma is a good name for her,' I told Mother, 'She's neither transcendental nor orderly.'

'You're assuming 'transcendental order' implies peaceful, quiet, and dull', she replied. 'Storms, earthquakes and diseases are all part of the natural order of things. I think it's a very appropriate name.'

Of course, there's no literal English translation of

Dharma. It's one of those complex concepts that loses its essence in translation, becoming fodder for new age hippies and inspirational plaques. Within the Western philosophical tradition, the closest comparable term is Spinoza's 'Deus sive natura' or the Hegelian Absolute, neither of which are particularly good names for cats.

I often wonder if she was already beginning to sense her time was running out. The first symptoms of her declining health started to show, although they were subtle to begin with. She would return from a camping trip exhausted, or overdo her gardening, or catch a cold from one of her students, and spend the following week sick in bed. Each time she visited her doctor, he would take a blood test, and each time it would show a slight increase of creatinine, symptomatic of the slow death of her transplanted kidney.

None of her ailments were serious, but they were notably regular. As soon as she recovered, she would launch into some new adventure. The camping trips grew longer and bolder, the educational reforms more sweeping, and the gardening grander. Whenever she fell ill, her girlfriend would make a point of launching into a melodramatic tantrum, keeping her up late into the night.

One winter Mother contracted bronchitis so badly she was sent to hospital where she acquired a pseudomonas chest infection. After she was released, her doctors demanded she sit in the kitchen for a half hour each day, breathing into a portable ventilator. A long tube hung from the ventilator, extending out through an open window, so as to pump the bacteria in her lungs out of the house. For a period of weeks, she was unable to work, garden, or go camping.

It was in this period that her girlfriend cheated on her and they broke up. It was to be her last love affair; a mid-life blossom rather than the start of a fine old age. After her death, I found several journals filled with anguished and heart- broken poetry on the topic:

> I miss her and our love that's gone. I'm boring and
> needy, so I'm alone.

I don't think Mother was surprised at how the relationship ended but she was uncharacteristically miserable for several months. It was not a mood I had seen in her before, or at least not for any extended period of time. I was not sure how to respond.

A few months later, her doctors noticed a series of calcified glands clustered in her throat. They had to be surgically removed, and for a week she had a long, jagged cut across her neck, held together by black stitches. For some reason, the surgeon left the stitches loose at the ends. We went out to dinner, where Mother made a point of pulling the thread back and forth. 'Look what I can do,' she laughed.

'I don't think you should do that.'

Although she was still only in her fifties, I mark this as the start of her old age. She had only a decade left to live and her best years had already passed.

22

> The Edwardian knut was never an angry young man. He would get a little cross, perhaps, if his man Meadows sent him out some morning with odd spats on, but his normal outlook on life was sunny. He was a humble, kindly soul who knew he was a silly ass and hoped you wouldn't mind. — P. G. Wodehouse

As Mother grew into premature old age, I became a man in the social, rather than legal or biological sense. I achieved this partly by mimicking the behaviour of my lecturers, and partly by reading P. G. Wodehouse novels. The latter were particularly important. I found about thirty of them in the remainder bin at my local bookstore, and read them all.

Wodehouse's books are full of delightful Edwardian idiots. His protagonists are usually young bachelors from the leisured classes, always well-intentioned but inept. I liked them because they were the opposite of the boys I knew growing up. They were not angry, or cruel, or sexist. Their world was sweet, harmless, and funny.

At university I felt very much like an outsider and thought P. G. Wodehouse might help me fit in. My peers and lecturers were nearly all from the middle and owning classes, and I found them very hard to understand. From his characters, I learned the importance of dress and mannerisms. I stopped wearing t-shirts and shorts, and started wearing button-up shirts and slacks. I began speaking as softly as possible and apologising a lot.

The dividends were significant. Shopkeepers addressed me as 'sir', passing youths no longer threatened to kick my head in, and my peers started inviting me to social events. Within a few months, I began my second, more serious, romance, with a woman who lived in one of the better suburbs on the other side of town.

She had a large and cheerful family, who invited me to their regular gatherings, and spoke jubilantly about food, wine, and family affairs. We made friends with other young couples, attended dinner parties, and went on weekends away. Wherever we went, people were nice to us. It was my first real encounter with the heterosexual world.

When people hear about my parentage, they're often surprised I turned out straight. There's an assumption that homosexual parents are more likely to produce homosexual children. I've never seen any proof of this, although I suppose if you grow up with homosexuals you're less likely to become closeted in later life.

That's not to say Mother's sexuality had no lasting impact. As a boy, I had experienced the bigotries and barriers she faced. As a man, these barriers suddenly dissolved, and yet I could still feel their imprint. At twenty-three, when I followed my new girlfriend through those various dinner parties and family functions, I saw for the first time a world devoid of many of the stresses I had taken for granted.

The further I went into that world, the further Mother and I were drawn apart. We didn't talk about it until she was dying and, even then, we could only do so indirectly. 'Do you remember when Dennis died?' she asked me.

'Of course I do.'

I had been halfway through my honours year, working on my thesis. We had him put down because he was old, frail, and had cancer. As the vet gave him the injection, we held him and sobbed as he passed out of our lives.

'The day afterwards,' Mother told me, 'I walked outside barefoot and trod in one of his poos. It made me cry. He was such a good dog.'

'And then I moved out?'

'Yes, then you moved out. And I cried then as well. I didn't want you to go, but I knew you were ready.'

I was surprised because I had not thought myself ready. Also, I thought she wanted the house to herself. 'I thought you were relieved,' I told her.

'I was, but I was also sad.'

I did not move far away, renting a small maisonette in a neighbouring suburb. My girlfriend lived with me for a while, but then decided she was going to study overseas. I thought she would come back, and we would settle down, but she didn't. Instead, we spent a year trying to have a long-distance relationship and I began a long period of living alone.

Mother and I saw each other two or three times a week. I was still working part-time at the nursing home, and most of my income went into rent, so she bought me dinner and took me shopping. She became almost embarrassingly proud of me.

'He's working so hard.' she would tell her friends, 'He's just finished reading *Ulysses*. And he's written a very good honours thesis on post-colonialism.'

At that age, I was working hard, although mostly I laboured

in vain. I did not understand *Ulysses* in the slightest, and my honours thesis was enthusiastic but lacklustre. At the end of the year, I was offered a position in the doctoral program, but no scholarship.

'Do you need a scholarship?' Mother asked me.

'Well, I think it's expected. But no, I don't think you need one,' I told her.

I enrolled in the doctoral program, intending to write a new history of the novel, the first of a number of Sisyphean tasks I set myself during my twenties.

With my girlfriend studying overseas, and rent consuming the bulk of my income, I took on extra hours at the nursing home, but the pay was so low it didn't make much difference. I decided I needed some sort of trade so I enrolled in a librarianship course, which I worked on alongside my PhD. It was an extremely stressful time, although Mother was very impressed by my industry.

Once I'd finished the librarianship course, I took up a weekend job working at a public library in the outer suburb of Elizabeth. It was a strange place, master planned in the 1960s, and described by Robyn Boyd as 'a horizontal slice of pure contemporary Australia, all the best and worst of it.' By the time I started work there, it had attained a reputation for serial killers, gang violence, and intergenerational poverty.

I began working there the same week Pope John Paul II died. On my first day, when I arrived at the train station, someone had spray painted 'The Pope Smokes Dope' on the wall in homage.

During my first shift, I struck up a conversation with one of my colleagues. 'What are you studying?' he asked me.

'Well. I'm trying to write a history of the novel.'

'That sounds like a load of wank.'

After my shift, I returned to the train station to find the memorial to the Pope's dope smoking had received an addendum. One of the local wits had added 'And look what happened to him!' in smaller letters.

At the time, I was trying to write a chapter on Joseph Conrad's *Heart of Darkness*. On the train, going back and forth between my shifts, I read Edward Said's *Culture and Imperialism*, with his description of Conrad as the first 'self-conscious' colonial author, and then Chinua Achebe's critique of him as a 'purveyor of comforting myths.' I thought they were both brilliant.

I wanted to write something similar; about suburbs and imperialism, although I couldn't figure out exactly what I was trying to say. Each day, as I headed to and from the library, I would study the opening passages of *Heart of Darkness*:

> The conquest of the earth, which mostly means the taking it away from those who have a different complexion or slightly flatter noses than ourselves, is not a pretty thing when you look into it too much. What redeems it is the idea only. The idea at the back of it; not a sentimental pretence but an idea… something you can set up, and bow down before…

The train would rumble through stations with British names: Elizabeth, Salisbury, and Regency Park, and then through rows of sun-bleached houses, punctuated by tarmacked streets, telephone poles, traffic lights, and fish and chip shops.

I never did complete my chapter, although I spent a lot of time thinking about it. When I visited Mother, I would try to articulate my thoughts. 'Do you think there's some redeeming idea behind it all?' I asked, 'Something you can bow down to?'

'Behind what?'

'Behind all this,' I said, gesturing around me, 'Do you think Flinders Park was built with some greater idea in mind?'

We were walking alongside the river, which sparkled with the oily gleam of the surrounding roads. She stopped and looked about her. 'Well people certainly seem to enjoy having ideas,' she offered, 'so probably some of them have a redeeming quality. I've got an idea to put a new mandarin tree down the back of the yard, which I think is quite good. I need you to come to Bunnings with me and pick up the tree and a few sacks of manure.'

Although she had always wanted to live alone, she had never actually done so and I think she was lonely. After her break-up, with Dennis gone, and me out of the house, whole days went by when she spoke only to Dharma, who remained distinctly feral.

I wasn't surprised when she rang me one afternoon to announce she had acquired a new dog. She referred to him as a 'curly coated retriever cross', although the 'cross' clearly dominated his breeding.

'I'm going to call him Arthur,' she told me.

Arthur had been rescued from the local pound, and must have endured some trauma in his youth as he was an extremely nervous little dog. Whenever I tried to talk about Conrad, Mother would interrupt me, and redirect the conversation towards him.

'Achebe says Conrad's work is all about the anxiety of the

West.'

'I think Arthur has an anxiety disorder. When he gets scared he hides in my bed and wets himself. I had to change the sheets five times last night.'

After about two weeks, Mother began to confuse the two of us. 'I took Ianto for a walk and he lost his tennis ball. When I found it, he was so happy he did one of his dances for five whole minutes. I had to give him a biscuit to make him stop.'

Arthur and I did have a lot in common. Like me, he had a long list of phobias: the sound of large trucks, bicycles, the postman, large open spaces, and men over a certain height. One afternoon he got a bee caught in his tail hair and was, forever after, afraid of buzzing insects. Sometimes when the wind caught his tail hair he would panic and begin to yip and spin in circles.

'Am I really as nervous as him?' I asked my mother.

'You've developed better coping mechanisms,' she told me. 'But he's a lot younger than you are, so I'm hoping he'll grow into himself, just like you.'

He never did. Fortunately, he never had to as she indulged his fears with far more patience than she had mine. Indeed, I think she found his adoring dependence gave her something weak against which to measure her own strength. I did not understand this at the time because I considered her to be indefatigable and free from doubt. In this, I now see, I was mistaken.

23

> [Y]ou will observe an island to the south of these Straits called Singapura; this is the spot, the ancient maritime capital of the Malays… on which I have planted the British flag… — Sir Stamford Raffles

At the age of twenty-four, I finally secured a scholarship to complete my doctorate. By then, I knew I would never be an academic. No matter how many P. G. Wodehouse novels I read, there was always a part of university life that made no sense. Still, when I told Mother, she unexpectedly burst into tears.

'It's not really that important,' I explained, 'lots of idiots get scholarships.'

'It's not the scholarship,' she told me. 'It's everything that came before it.'

I quit both my jobs and spent two glorious years studying without interruption. It felt like something had shifted, as if I had moved out of one world and into another.

Mother began calling me regularly to offer life advice, usually focused on my health. I couldn't understand what she was talking about. One afternoon, she rang me four times in three hours, each time to suggest I get tested for heart disease. 'Both your grandfathers had heart attacks, and your father died young,' she explained, 'You might be at risk of a heart attack.'

'I don't think I'm going to have a heart attack. I'm only twenty-four, I don't drink, and I'm a vegetarian who rides a bicycle every day.'

'Yes, but your father died young.'

'But he smoked, drank, ate too much, and never exercised. And he didn't have a heart attack, he had an aneurism.'

At first, I thought she had some legitimate concern for my health. I even went to a doctor, who looked at me like I was an idiot, took a blood test, and confirmed I was not at risk of having a heart attack.

When I explained this to Mother she went quiet for a few days, and then began a new line of enquiry. 'I've been thinking about your cholesterol levels, and I think you should start eating fish.'

'Good grief Mother, I'm not having another conversation about heart disease. Let's change the subject.'

There was a pause. 'I spoke to my ex today,' she said. 'And I told her she was a jerk.'

'Why did you do that?'

'Well, she is a jerk.'

I agreed with her but it had been more than a year since their separation and it seemed like a moot point.

Over the following weeks, she stopped talking about my heart and fixated on her ex's many character flaws. I was confused as I had never known her to dwell on anything, other than her garden, for any length of time. Even her sporadic furies against my grandmother rarely lasted more than a week.

Things came to a head when she unexpectedly won the top prize in the Kidney Foundation's annual charity raffle, which she had entered every year since her transplant without success.

'It's a two-week international travel package,' she told me, 'I thought we could go overseas together.'

For a few weeks, she stopped complaining about her ex and we talked about the various places she wanted to visit.

'I've always wanted to go to London,' she said. 'I suppose it seems like the quintessential holiday destination. We could go to Kew Gardens.'

Unfortunately, her doctors thought long distance travel was too dangerous. They spent a long time telling her about water borne infections, deep vein thrombosis, and Avian influenza. 'They say I need to be within six flying hours of home, in case something goes wrong with my kidney.'

This ruled out Europe and the United States. The bulk of Asia was out because her doctors thought poor water quality might play havoc with her health. Eventually we settled on Singapore, on account of its extremely high standards of hygiene and world class health system.

The raffle had been organised on the assumption its top prize would be won by a couple. All the pamphlets from the travel agency promised 'romantic getaways'. When we arrived at the hotel they had booked us into a single room, into which they hastily installed a second bed. We had not slept in the same room for years and, on the first night, I discovered Mother had developed a mammoth snoring problem. Every half hour or so, she would cease breathing altogether for ten or fifteen seconds and then emit a noise like the roaring of a bear.

'I'm sorry dear,' she explained. 'It's because of that lung infection I had.'

The pseudomonas in her lungs had left behind a mass of viscous fluid which could not be removed. The snoring was but one of numerous respiratory side effects she had accumulated without my knowledge. She also had a new and persistent cough, frequent shortness of breath, and occasional bouts of giddiness. Her skin, I noticed, had become brittle and prone to bruising.

Over breakfast, she went through her usual process of sorting, then taking, the medications she needed for her kidney: cortisone, prednisone, and a variety of brightly-coloured immune-suppressants. Among the familiar bottles and blister packs I noticed an addition, marked 'Serotonin'.

'What are you taking that for?' I asked.

'It's because I had those glands cut out of my neck.' 'But isn't serotonin an anti-depressant?'

She launched into a lengthy analysis of the relationship between the body's various glands, little of which I understood. 'My cortisone tablets caused my parathyroid glands to calcify, and that put my hormones out of synch, so now I don't have enough serotonin.'

'So this means you're getting depressed?'

'It means my glands aren't producing serotonin.'

'Isn't depression the major side effect of low serotonin?'

'My glands don't produce enough serotonin,' she repeated.

She certainly didn't seem depressed. Of course, neither of us had been overseas before, and were both filled with a childish excitement. We wandered between temples, shrines, shopping malls, and public parks, admiring the crowds and the sparkling clean mass transit system. The British had arrived in Singapore about the same time they'd arrived in South Australia. It had the same straight and orderly streets, neoclassical buildings, and bridges named after long-dead imperialists.

One afternoon, we took the cable car to Sentosa Island to visit the gigantic statue of Singapore's totem animal, the

'Merlion': half lion, half fish, and built entirely of fibreglass. In its tail, we found a small gift shop, where we were offered the opportunity to ascend into the Merlion's mighty head and have our photo taken within its jaws. I still have the photograph, with both of us grinning broadly against the backdrop of the city's port, the horizon dotted by a long stream of container ships.

'Actually, I'm quite glad I'm here with you and not with my ex,' Mother told me. 'She'd only be whinging about something.'

We took the lift back down from the Merlion's mouth, and wandered along the beach until we found a man selling coconuts with colourful straws sticking out of them. We drank them on the foreshore, watching the container ships unloading.

'Do you think the lack of serotonin has anything to do with why you talk about your ex so much?' I asked her.

I expected her to ignore the question, but she seemed surprised. 'Do I talk about her a lot?'

'Yes. It's like you got over her, and then stopped being over her, and now you either talk about her, or about me having a heart attack.'

There was another pause. 'I suppose it's not so much the break-up,' she told me, 'I suppose I'm starting to feel a bit old.'

She was fifty-six and I had not thought of her as old, but when I look back at the pictures of our trip I see she is stooped over and her skin is papery and blotched.

'Do you think that's why you're feeling depressed, or is it just the serotonin?' I asked her.

She considered the question for several moments, without offering a response.

'I suppose the two aren't mutually exclusive,' I offered.

'No. I suppose they're not.'

There was another extended pause before she continued. 'When you're young, when something happens, you can tell yourself you'll get over it, so you think about the future,' she told me. 'But after a certain point, you can't tell yourself that anymore.'

I thought through what she was saying. 'So, are you worried about the future?'

'Well, not at the moment, because we're on holiday, and you're here and I know if anything went wrong you'd be there.'

I had, of course, thought a good deal about her death but the death of a loved one is entirely different to the onset of old age. There's a simplicity to someone being dead, whereas the fragility of old age offers an infinite array of confronting complications.

We both sat in silence for some minutes until Mother changed the subject.' How much longer is your girlfriend going to be overseas?'

'She says a year.'

At that point, it had become a fairly empty shell of an affair. 'What will you do when she gets back?'

'I suppose I'll finish my thesis, get a job in a library, and we'll settle down together.'

'Is that what you want to do?'

I contemplated the question. 'I suppose it seems inevitable.'

'That's not correct,' she declared, 'You always have a choice.'

'Did you have a choice with your ex?'

'I didn't have a choice about her cheating on me. But I made a choice to put up with it as long as I did.'

'Do you regret it?'

'No,' she said, 'Regret isn't the right word. I wish she hadn't been such a colossal turd but I can't control that. It's the paradox of life. You're defined by your own decisions, but your decisions are defined by things you have no control over.'

'That sounds pretty depressing.'

'Maybe, but you have to remember it's a choice to not make a decision, so I think it's probably better for you to act like you are in control. I think if you've stopped making decisions you've probably stopped wanting to be alive. I haven't stopped wanting to make decisions, I just don't have as much control over the decisions I make.'

Years later, I found her photographs from the trip, most of which she had taken surreptitiously while she trailed after me through the streets of Singapore. In shot after blurry shot, I appear clutching my map and guiding us between the various tourist locales, as she watches me walk on ahead.

24

> I am not a drop-out; I was never in. I have not spent my life hacking my way through the constraints of bourgeois existence. I was always free – appallingly free. — Quentin Crisp

When we arrived back in Adelaide, I broke up with my girlfriend and finished my doctorate. I worked in a library for a while, but quit to pursue a variety of art projects, none of which were financially or aesthetically successful. Mother was extremely proud of me and, when we went out for dinner or walked Arthur along the river, she made a point of telling me so.

'I'm so proud of you. You're taking such wonderful risks.'

Most of my energy went into trying to establish a variety of utopian art spaces, all of which devolved into semi-legal nightclubs, catering to an audience of impoverished alcoholics, depressives, and those local middle-class youths who had yet to move interstate. The risks related mostly to fines for breach of liquor licensing and fire regulations.

Still, I was approaching the age she had been when I was born, and living the kind of life she had wanted: unencumbered, alone, and free to do as I pleased. For my twenty-seventh birthday, she took me to see the play *Resident Alien*, based on the life of the writer and gay icon Quentin Crisp. The play portrayed him in his final years, living alone in a decrepit studio apartment, partially paralysed, and alternately lamenting and celebrating his irreconcilable eccentricity.

We both thought the play was wonderful. For Mother's birthday, I gave her a copy of his book, *The Naked Civil Servant*. In her card, I inscribed his famous comment on housekeeping:

> There is no need to do any housework at all. After the first four years the dirt doesn't get any worse.

She thought it was a wonderful gift, and kept the card on the window sill next to her bed.

By that time, I had filled my rented maisonette with old books and furniture dragged out of hard rubbish. It became infested with mice, whose nests I often discovered in my bookshelves. Later, their numbers were greatly reduced by a large lizard. I don't know how it got into the house, but it would gorge on baby mice and then fall asleep on my kitchen floor.

Mother visited regularly. She was very impressed by the lizard and by my housekeeping in general. For Christmas, she gave me a coconut with a ribbon stuck to it. 'Happy Christmas! I bought you a coconut, just like the ones we had in Singapore.'

I had no way of opening it, so the coconut sat in my refrigerator until it sprouted an interesting blue mould, which quickly spread from the crisper and into the various door compartments. Each time Mother visited we would inspect its progress. She referred to it as the 'Secret Garden.' It stayed like this for the better part of three years. I lived mostly on fresh fruit and bread.

I entered my thirties. My student debt was greater than my superannuation. My utopian art spaces barely paid their own rent. I had no money and all my friends had moved away. Every year I had a fleeting, doomed romance, which ended when the object of my affections moved interstate or overseas.

I had always been, like the rest of my family, a teetotaller, but I gave that up and spent many happy nights on the town, making friends with people who were too drunk or too poor to move interstate. After one such night, I woke up horribly hung over, threw up seven times, and then spent the whole day on the bathroom floor. As I lay there, I pictured myself in old age. I imagined myself in the same position, but with some real and incurable ailment. I realised that, after Mother's death, I would face such travails alone. At some point in the not-too-distant future, she would die and I would face all of life's petty hurdles alone. It struck me that I was unhappy.

Was Mother aware of this, I wonder? Probably she assumed my personality was inherently melancholic. I certainly wondered about her happiness, although she never again discussed her serotonin as anything other than a technical issue. Her health continued its slow decline. She grew tired quickly, caught every passing cold, and seemed to be napping whenever I called.

On the advice of her doctors, she left her stressful yet rewarding job at one of the state's foremost down-at-heel schools, and took up an ostensibly easier position close to home. Her new school was bland, and both parents and teachers were uniformly conservative. They were rarely open about their bigotry but it became quickly apparent. They made a series of complaints about the lack of tidiness in her classroom and the absence of colouring-in lessons.

Mother had no tolerance for them, and made no attempt to fit in. She arrived at work each day in the Van Dyke, with its rainbow coloured cat sticker and the canoe strapped to the roof, but she no longer boasted about the shock she caused. I noticed she spoke less and less about her work. Outside of working hours, she spent her time sleeping, gardening, or taking Arthur for walks along the river. When she was in her thirties, she had written in her diary:

> When I am old
> My mind will wander
> Around plants, water sprays,
> Slugs and new grass shoots.
> You'll find me talking to weeds.
> Yesterday I nodded 'Good morning' to a soursob.

Now she was in her sixties. She no longer had the energy to prune or fertilize as she once had and, as a result, the decorative plants died off and the weeds ran wild. In winter, the garden filled with soursobs and, in summer, with nasturtiums. I saw her speak to both.

'What a lovely colour you are. Although I wish you hadn't killed off those irises. They were very expensive.'

She spent as much time in the garden as she could. She stopped doing housework entirely. Dishes piled up in the sink, newspaper lay crumpled across the barren floorboards, clothes remained in the washing machine.

I asked if she wanted help, but she thought I was being pedantic. 'Do you want me to do the dishes for you?' I offered.

'No, but I do want you to come to Bunnings with me. I need help picking out some manure.'

The house became so messy even I began to feel she had

crossed a line. Dharma would only eat part of her daily meals and the remainder, left in her bowl atop the laundry cabinet, would go rancid. Arthur took empty cat food tins out of the bin and littered them throughout the house. I was in no position to criticise her, as my own house was filled with junk, mice, and the mouldy coconut.

Besides, she seemed happy. From the local second-hand stores, she accumulated large supplies of crockery, odd bits of furniture, and small knick-knacks. She scattered them throughout the house or placed them whimsically in the garden, where they were quickly consumed by the soursobs.

The neighbourhood around her began to change as well. The local council changed a by-law, allowing people to build two houses on a single block. After that, whenever one of the neighbours died, their house was bought by a developer, demolished, and replaced with two pre-fabricated cubes. These cubes were then advertised as 'modern family homes,' although they were mostly bought by retirees.

When her next-door neighbour died, Mother noticed their yard was cleared and a cube installed, but the original house remained untouched. She thought this was unusual until, one afternoon, the police conducted an extensive and spectacular raid.

'A police man came around and asked if I'd seen anything,' she told me. 'Apparently, the block was bought by a drug baron, who used the old house to grow hydroponic marijuana. He had some of his henchmen living in the cube, keeping an eye on things.'

After that, the cube was purchased by another drug dealer, who lived there with his family until he was arrested. 'It's a shame,' said Mother, 'they were a very nice family really.'

As the cube houses grew more numerous, flocks of wild birds began nesting in her garden. Dharma had no interest in them, but took infinite joy in seeing off the innumerable cats they attracted. The place became a sort of avian sanctuary.

One afternoon, Mother rang me to tell me she had found a chicken scratching about among a mound of flowering vines by the front tap. 'I've called her Cluck Cluck,' she said. 'I need you to come and help me build a coop for her.'

We spent an afternoon driving back-and-forth to Bunnings, building a chicken coop out of wire and bits of wood. I thought it was quite good, but Cluck Cluck didn't spend much time in it. 'She's a very sociable chicken,' Mother explained, 'and I don't think she likes being locked away.'

For the most part, Cluck Cluck was allowed to roam as she pleased. I often found her in the house, strutting about the kitchen or sitting on the arm of the sofa. 'I don't think you should let her in the house,' I told her. 'I don't think she's safe around Arthur.'

'Don't be silly. She, Arthur, and Dharma are all good friends. They often have breakfast together.'

From what I saw, Dharma avoided her, and Arthur thought she was terrifying. Cluck Cluck took food directly from his bowl while he stood quivering with frustration. She was a quarter his size but much more confident. Things went on like this for some weeks until one afternoon Mother called me, her voice breaking with emotion. 'Cluck Cluck is dead.' I did not say anything, although I could already guess the circumstances of her demise.

'I think she must have had a fight with Arthur. He's covered in feathers!' I cycled over to her house and we buried Cluck Cluck beneath the pepper tree. Afterwards, we went to the garden store and purchased more hardy ground covers to mark the grave.

Arthur was forgiven almost immediately, although I think the incident affected him more than we thought. He became very protective of my mother. I suspect he saw Cluck Cluck as a dangerous interloper she had been powerless to repel. When she took him out for his walks he attacked anyone who came near her, growling at pedestrians and chasing after cyclists. If anyone came into the yard, or even walked past on the footpath outside, he would fly into a fury.

He developed an intense hatred of the postman. When he delivered the mail each day, Arthur charged at the front gate, overcome with rage.

'I really think you need to be more careful,' I warned her. 'Arthur is getting very aggressive. If he bites someone you might have to have him put down.'

'I've discussed it with him and he's agreed he'll try to be better behaved.'

A week later, she left the front gate ajar, Arthur got out, and cornered the postman against the fence. 'It took me half an hour to calm them both down. Arthur wouldn't stop barking and the postman said he was going to lodge a formal complaint. He said Arthur was a dangerous dog.'

'I told you that you needed to be more careful.'

'I am careful. They were both being silly. After all, Arthur doesn't have any front teeth.'

This was true. He had worn them out chewing on tennis balls. Mother had explained this to the postman, who agreed he would let the incident drop if she promised to keep the gate shut in the future.

Arthur's defensiveness was misdirected, but not misguided. Mother was growing weaker, and she did struggle to protect herself. At her work, a small group of parents lodged a formal complaint against her, insisting she was unfit to be a teacher.

'They've complained to the principal,' she told me, 'but it wasn't clear what they were actually complaining about, so the complaint was dropped.' She was clearly struggling. When we went out walking she grew weary after ten or fifteen minutes. We often had to sit down while she caught her breath. 'Arthur says he needs a little rest,' she would say, and we would sit and watch the river before making our way home.

She saw her doctors once a month, and they measured her creatinine, serotonin, calcium, and protein levels. After one of her visits, we walked along the river until she sat down, with Arthur slumped beside her. 'The doctors told me I could apply for a disability pension,' she said.

'What did you say?'

'I must admit, I hadn't thought of myself as having a disability, but they say I fit all the criteria.'

'Do you feel disabled?'

'I'm not sure. What does disabled feel like?'

'What does able-bodied feel like?'

'That's a good question,' she replied. 'I suppose I don't feel able-bodied.' Yet she did not revisit the subject with her doctors and instead introduced a new curriculum of abstract math, causing no end of controversy at the mid-semester parent teacher interviews. From that point onwards, I began to worry about her more than she worried about me.

25

> Diana's shape and habit straight he took,
> Soften'd his brows, and smooth'd his awful look…
> — Ovid

As she approached her sixtieth birthday, Mother begrudgingly allowed her doctors to talk her into dropping down to a part-time position, albeit still at the same school. It was her first major admission that she could not live as she pleased. The conservative faction among the parents took it as a show of weakness and launched a steady campaign of complaints and innuendo.

She must have discussed the possibility of a disability pension with Gran, as the two of them began to argue the point. Several weeks of obtuse and ambiguous debate followed. After each episode, Mother rang me to complain. 'Your grandmother thinks I should retire, but she's got no right to tell me what to do.'

'I think Gran is just a bit worried.'

'I'm a grown woman! I can make my own decisions.'

A few days later they reached a compromise. 'I'm going to keep working,' Mother said, 'but I'm going to let her clean my house once a fortnight.'

It seemed a strangely one-sided compromise but Gran duly began driving down from the hills every second Saturday to spend an afternoon washing the dishes, doing the laundry, mopping the floors, and picking up the rubbish Arthur had dragged out of the bin. Usually, they would end the day with a mild tiff.

Gran was well into her eighties, and devoted most of her time to taking care of my grandfather, who had begun his descent into dementia. 'Are you sure Gran is up to doing all your cleaning?' I asked.

'It makes her feel better if I let her clean up,' she replied. 'So really, I'm doing her a favour.'

A month later, I received a call from my aunt, Merridy. 'I'm very concerned about your grandmother. She's exhausting herself.'

'With the cleaning? I thought Gran enjoyed it?'

'No. It takes her three days to recover. It makes her miserable.'

Merridy's solution was to join Gran on her fortnightly forays to Mother's house. It was hard to tell if this made things better or worse. When I asked her how it was going, she sounded flustered. 'I usually wash the floors, do the dishes and the laundry, and then pick up all the rubbish Arthur has taken out of the kitchen bin. And the two of them follow me about and explain how I'm doing it wrong.'

'They seem to be arguing less.'

'Yes, because they're both busy yelling at me.'

Every fortnight, I called Mother and then Merridy, one after the other. Their stories were never the same.

'They had a lovely time,' Mother would announce, 'I let them potter about for an hour or two, and then I made them go for a walk and we got fish and chips.'

When I rang my aunt, she would tell me the opposite. 'The two of them spent the whole time bickering. I spent an hour scrubbing the floors. I did the floors last fortnight as well, but they were filthy! Then Dimity made me get her fish and chips. And then she dropped the wrapping on the floor! I think she's deliberately making more mess. She seems to think we enjoy cleaning up after her.'

She was right. When I visited Mother, she let me help her with the shopping but grew irritable if I tried to do any cleaning. 'No, no! Leave that for Merridy! She'll be very upset if there's not a good pile of dishes for her to do.'

One Friday night I went to Mother's house for dinner, and found a long stream of dirt running from the front door, through the living room, and into the kitchen, where it ended in a pool of mud.

'What happened here?'

'I bought a twelve-litre bag of potting soil, but it was too heavy to lift out of the car, so I shovelled it into a bucket and carried it through the house to the back garden. Except the bucket had a hole in it, so some of the soil leaked out. And then I dropped the bucket in the kitchen and it went everywhere. Your aunt and your grandmother are going to have a wonderful time tomorrow.'

I called Merridy the next afternoon and she was on the cusp of tears. 'I think you should hire a cleaner,' I told Mother.

I thought this might settle some of the tension. It did not. On the contrary, Mother became cagey and defensive. 'I don't need a cleaner!' she protested.

'I think it's too much work for Gran.'

'Well, I only let her do it as a favour. She doesn't have to do it. I certainly didn't ask her to.'

I think she suspected I had been colluding with my aunt. We argued the point for three months. Every few weeks she would relent and agree to a cleaner. Then, on the day they were due to arrive, she would cancel them at the last moment.

'Why did you cancel?' I would ask.

'I was too tired to have someone fussing about the house. Plus it makes your grandmother happy when I let her do my cleaning.'

Part of me believed her. I could see she was struggling but I still thought of her as I had when I was a boy. It was unfathomable that she could need help. When I did her shopping, or my aunt cleaned her floors, I accepted she was doing us a favour; that she was making a concession to our concern, and not her failing health.

That winter, Mother caught a long series of colds and her doctors began discussing the disability pension with increased frequency and force. She seemed tired all the time, and strangely confused. Later, I realised these were the symptoms of kidney failure. Her blood was growing thick with toxins and thin in oxygen, making it hard for her to think clearly.

The Van Dyke became her next major concession. She began calling every month or so to announce she had crashed it into something. Initially, she presented these accidents as comic misadventures. 'I met the most fascinating person today. I backed the van into his car and we had quite a good chat.'

Over time, I began to notice the stories had a predictable formula: she would back into someone's car, they would get upset, and she would somehow convince them it was their fault because their vehicle was grey and thus invisible, or they were driving impatiently. Once this was accomplished, she declared the damage minor, the weather beautiful, and dragged them into a conversation about gardening.

Gran saw through this faster than I did. She launched a campaign to convince Mother to sell the Van Dyke and buy a smaller car with power steering and fewer blind spots.

'She still thinks I'm a child,' Mother protested. 'But I'm going to be driving the van until I'm eighty! I'm going to drive around the country.'

A few weeks later, she rang to say Arthur had asked her to sell the Van Dyke. When I asked her why, she explained he was having trouble jumping into it. He was getting old and had begun to suffer from arthritis of the hips.

'He thinks I should get something a bit smaller, and lower to the ground, with power steering and fewer blind spots,' she explained.

'Isn't that what Gran suggested?'

'The vet says Arthur has some arthritic tendencies in his hips and jumping in and out of the van makes them worse.'

Several weeks later, she let slip the real story. She had been driving through a roundabout near our house when she found herself suddenly and unexpectedly stopped. After some minutes, she noticed another car pressed against the Van Dyke's bonnet. For a brief and terrifying moment she thought she had killed someone. Mother only admitted this once and afterwards reverted to claiming she had sold the Van Dyke because of Arthur's arthritic hips.

I had hoped she might follow Gran's advice and purchase a smaller car but instead she bought a gigantic sedan. She kept a small wooden box in the back seat so Arthur could climb in and out more comfortably. 'I suppose I won't be driving around Australia. But at least your grandmother is happy.'

It was around this time I met Diana. The first time I saw her she was performing an experimental art work, centred mostly on eating bananas until she vomited. It was, she told me, influenced by Julia Kristeva's theories of the abject. I was deeply impressed. She lived in Sydney but spent two weeks in Adelaide, vomiting on herself each night. The rest of the time we spent together.

When she left, I spent several days moping. In this respect, the relationship followed the pattern of my previous romances. However, after a month, when the moping had not ended, I invested my meagre savings on a flight to Sydney, and stayed with her in her inner-city neighbourhood full of quaint terraces and art deco apartments. Occasionally, as we wandered through the irrationally weaving streets, I would glimpse the harbour.

When I returned to my house in Adelaide, I found the coconut had developed hardened tendrils. These were pressing against the fridge door, as if launching a bid to escape. I dragged the fridge onto the curb for hard rubbish collection and began, surreptitiously, to think of moving away.

As if in simpatico, Mother developed her own fixation with moving house. She had our home in Flinders Park valued and began spending her Saturdays reviewing the real estate pages in the paper. 'I'm thinking of downsizing,' she said, 'because the bedroom is too far away from the back door and Arthur often needs to go to the toilet in the night.'

As much as I lamented the loss of our family home, I could see her point. The house had always been a cheerful mess, but it was beginning to take on the sort of grim clutter one sees in documentaries about hoarders. Even with my aunt and grandmother's fortnightly crusades, there always seemed to be mounds of dishes in the sink, stale laundry in the washing machine, and rubbish scattered about the place. If she moved somewhere a bit smaller, I thought, I might not have to worry so much and could perhaps consider moving to Sydney.

Mother started spending her weekends at house inspections. Initially, she looked at smaller town houses or maisonettes, closer to the city and the hospital. Gran, Merridy, and I all thought these sounded quite sensible. Over time, however, she began looking at places that were larger than her current house, further away into the depths of the suburbs, and with even bigger gardens.

Eventually, she called to announce she wasn't moving after all. 'I was sitting in the garden, and the sun was coming through the leaves and I thought "If I leave, what will happen to all the birds?" So, I've decided to stay.'

A few weeks later, she began looking at the real estate pages again and the cycle would repeat itself. Eventually, we convinced her to let us do a major spring clean. We thought this might help her decide one way or the other. The three of us spent an entire weekend mopping, dusting, and collecting Arthur's half-chewed pieces of rubbish.

Mother spent the time following us about complaining. Afterwards, however, she produced a packet of expensive ice creams from the refrigerator and gave one to each of us as a reward. 'It looks lovely,' she admitted. When she finished her ice cream, she dropped the wrapper on the living room floor.

'I just mopped that floor.' Merridy protested.

'That's okay. Arthur will clean it up.' Arthur picked up the wrapper and retreated to the couch, where he proceeded to tear it into tiny pieces.

Gran and I took our ice creams out into the garden. 'I hear you're seeing a very nice girl in Sydney.'

'Yes. Her name is Diana. I think she's very nice.'

'Diana. Like that Roman myth. Does she own any dogs?'

'No, I don't think so.'

'That's a shame. But you think she's quite nice?'

'Yes, very nice.'

Gran paused, and then gestured back towards the house. 'Don't stay here because of this,' she told me.

The following week Mother and I went out for dinner. We had our usual discussion about her moving house. 'Arthur gets sore walking all the way from the bed down to the doggy door. I think I should get a house with a little courtyard next to the bedroom. Maybe a little maisonette in the city somewhere.'

'I think that's a good idea.'

'But then I sit in the backyard and look at all the little birds and think, "What would happen to them if I left?" And then I think I'd better stay.'

'Okay.'

We sat in silence. I was not eager to begin another discussion on the house. I suppose she didn't want to either. When she spoke again, it was on an entirely different topic. 'I'd miss you if you moved to Sydney,' she said, 'But I think you should go.'

'I'd miss you as well.' We fell back into silence. I felt as though I was going to cry.

'I don't think staying here is very good for you,' she continued. 'And if you move, I can visit you and we can ride the ferries together.'

I suppose by that point I was conscious of the distance between us, although I couldn't articulate it. Sometimes I wonder if the way I lived, alone with my coconut and my failing art spaces, was an attempt to keep us together, or at least an attempt to show her that I could live as she had wanted to live. Yet it wasn't just the obvious differences of class or gender pulling us apart; it was the sense that I had a future and she did not.

26

Full are thy cities with the sons of Art;
And trade and joy, in every busy street…
The palace stone, looks gay. Thy crowded ports
Where rising masts an endless prospect yield…
— James Thomson

I spent a week in Sydney looking at rental properties with Diana. Our budget was scant, and our options limited to lightless boxes and decrepit hovels. We settled on a dilapidated two-room terrace in Surry Hills, built in the 1860s and altered little since then. We were the only applicants and signed the lease on the last day of my visit.

'It's just been re-painted,' the landlord told us, 'And it's waterproof. Although the window seal leaks a bit. You can pick up the keys in a fortnight.'

'I noticed there was no door on the bathroom,' said Diana.

'Do you need a door?'

We went to a bar to celebrate. While we were there, Mother rang me. 'When are you coming back to Adelaide?' she asked.

'Tomorrow,' I told her. 'We've just signed a lease for a little terrace. It's a bit shabby but very cute.'

'Well that sounds nice.' There was a brief pause. 'Do you think you could feed Dharma for me next week?'

'Why do you need me to feed your cat?'

'I've had a heart attack. I have to stay in hospital for a few days.' She sounded nonplussed.

'Are you all right?'

'Oh yes, I'm fine. It was quite minor, so I didn't call you.'

'What happened?'

'I was home by myself and my arm went numb, so I looked up heart attack symptoms on the internet and called the ambulance. They arrived before it really got going, so the doctors say it's not too bad. But I need to stay here a bit longer.'

'When did it happen?'

'Three days ago.'

'Why didn't you tell me?'

'There wasn't anything I needed you to do.'

The following morning, I flew back to feed her cat. Afterwards, I went to the hospital. She was in a room by herself, propped up in bed, happily eating soup.

'How are you?' I asked.

'This soup is delicious.'

A doctor appeared in the doorway, clutching a clip board tightly to his chest. He looked younger than me and very nervous. Mother looked up from her soup and frowned, 'What do you want?'

'Mrs Ware,' he said, looking at the clipboard. 'How are you feeling today?'

'Ms. Not Mrs. I'm feeling quite good. Did you phone my renal specialist?'

'Oh, I'm sorry.'

'You need to phone my renal specialist. I told the duty nurse you'd talk to her about the results before she finished her shift.'

'When does she finish her shift?'

'She finished five minutes ago, but she's still out there so you'll catch her if you hurry.'

He scurried off. A few minutes later, the duty nurse stormed in. The doctor trailed after her, still clutching his clipboard. 'Sorry Dimity,' she said, 'I've just phoned the renal specialist but they've already left for the day so I don't have the results.'

Mother looked at the doctor, and he looked at the ground, shifting his weight from foot to foot. 'Sorry,' he said, 'I'll ring them first thing in the morning.'

The results were inconclusive. Mother was sent off for further tests. After a week, the renal specialist came to see her. He had spoken to a cardiac specialist and they had concluded the arteries around her heart were filled with hardened calcium, another side effect of the medication she took for her transplanted kidney.

'It's the same problem I had with those glands in my neck,' she told me.

'What are they going to do?'

'Normally,' she explained, 'they get a little drill and drill out the blockages. But they need to give me a general anaesthetic to do that, which they think will kill my kidney.'

Instead, they gave her a complex array of blood thinners and discharged her. My aunt Merridy and I took her home, where we discovered her fridge was completely empty. Mother sent Merridy off to the supermarket to buy a large box of ice creams.

'You need more than ice creams,' I told her. 'You need to get some proper food.'

'Ice creams are proper food,' she protested.

I stayed with her for the next two weeks, sleeping on a fold out bed in the spare room. During the days, I packed up my maisonette. I dragged my furniture out for hard rubbish, and put everything else into boxes. At night, I walked Arthur, cooked vegetables for Mother, and listened to her complain about my grandmother.

'She wants me to get a gardener. But I'm a grown woman! I like the garden the way it is.'

'Why does she want you to get a gardener?'

'Because she doesn't understand I'm a grown woman.'

I called Merridy, who gave me a different explanation. 'When she had the heart attack, the ambulance crew couldn't get to the front door. Apparently, the gurney got caught in some vines by the front gate. Your grandmother thinks she should hire a gardener to clear all the paths.'

That afternoon, I found Mother sitting in a lawn chair in the front yard, clutching the garden hose and looking ill.

'What happened?'

'Your grandmother was going on about gardeners again, so I hung up on her. Then I came out here to move some pots around and had an angina attack.'

'Do you think Gran has a point?'

She did not respond, but the next morning she called Gran again. She did not agree to hire a gardener but she did agree to a 'clean-up.' She spent the afternoon calling her friends. 'I told them my mother was in a mood,' she told me. 'So, they've offered to organise a working bee.'

That weekend, a small army of silver haired lesbians filled the yard, each carrying an array of pruning implements. They spent two days hacking through the undergrowth, trimming back the foliage, and clearing the paths.

Too weak to contribute, Mother spent the time propped up

in a lawn chair, clutching a garden hose with a high-pressure attachment. From this vantage point she blasted water at every plant in a three-metre radius and issued instructions in the voice she usually reserved for her classroom.

Some of her friends suggested the clean-up might be more effective if she wasn't around. Accordingly, on the second day I drove her down to the mouth of the river, where the water ran, brown and rank, into the ocean. She was too ill to walk along the shore so we sat in the sand dunes and watched earth movers dumping sand to make a storm break. Below us, a small boy stood with his father, watching them in open-mouthed wonder.

'You used to be just like that,' she told me.

I moved to Sydney a week later. Diana and I quickly discovered our terrace house was not waterproof after all. She had just started her doctorate, and I was only working part-time. We could not afford to move. Every few days, Mother would ring me to proclaim, 'I was just thinking it would be nice to go out to dinner. So, I thought I'd ring you up instead.'

For a while, I worried she regretted me leaving but the opposite seemed to be true. I think I was beginning to join the ranks of my grandmother and my aunt: constantly trying to help her, constantly making her feel she could not cope on her own. She could tolerate it from them but my pity made her feel weak.

Her health had not improved. The blood thinners lessened the stress on her heart, but made her foggy and confused. She allowed her doctors to lodge an application for a disability pension.

'I suppose I can't go back to work,' she told me. 'I wasn't really enjoying it and retirement does sound quite nice.'

Three months later, I flew back to Adelaide again, bringing Diana with me. We stayed with Mother, sleeping in the spare bedroom. I had hoped the two of them might develop some sort of relationship but Mother was in a strange, almost aggressively cheerful, mood. She followed Diana around, offering a deluge of suggestions on things we might like to see around the neighbourhood: a new hardware store in the next suburb, a family of geese nesting in a near-by park.

'I'm sorry,' I explained, 'she's not normally like this.'

'It is a bit full on,' Diana compained. 'I was on the toilet, and she was standing outside talking about geese. I wasn't sure what to say.'

I thought perhaps Mother had simply been spending too much time alone, so we took her out on day trips: to the museum, the art gallery, and into the botanic gardens. One afternoon, we took her to the beach, where heavy surf pounded the shore. She announced she had forgotten her heart medication, stripped to her underpants, and waded in. 'It's perfect weather for body surfing,' she declared.

Diana asked if we should stop her but I knew that we could not. Instead, we stood on the shore, watching her tumble about in the swell. After fifteen minutes, she emerged, soaked and panting for breath. 'You didn't want to swim?' she asked us.

'It looks a bit rough, Dimity,' Diana told her. 'Do you want us to go and get your heart medication?'

'No, but I think we need to get some fish and chips. South Australian fish and chips are much fresher than the ones you get in Sydney.'

After six months, her doctors concluded her medication was not working and she was admitted to hospital to have the worst of the arterial blockages cleared.

She rang me after the operation. 'It was a success. I feel better already.'

'What about your kidney?'

'The doctors say I can go home next week.'

I flew back to Adelaide again, this time on my own. To my surprise, Mother came to the airport to pick me up. She had lost weight, and her skin was pale, but she was very cheerful. We drove to an Indian restaurant her friend Karen had recommended.

Over dinner, she suddenly presented her wrist to me, adorned with a new, freshly healed scar. 'Look. I have a new fistula,' she announced. 'Touch it.'

When I placed my finger upon it I could feel the pulse of her heart. The doctors, she explained, had used the opportunity of her heart operation to stitch together an artery and a vein in her wrist.

'This,' she explained, 'is where they'll pump the blood in and out when I go back on dialysis.'

This was not to be her only surprise. When we got home, she lifted up her shirt to reveal a piece of plastic tubing dangling from a bandaged wound in her belly. The doctors had installed a stent into her stomach, allowing for an alternate form of dialysis in which fluid was drained through her stomach cavity. I later discovered they had installed both stent and fistula because it was certain that one or the other would fail.

'So, I take it the operation damaged your kidney?' I asked.

'Yes, I thought I told you.'

'No, you didn't.'

'I would have liked a few more years but it will be nice to

have clean blood again.'

She was, to my surprise, quite optimistic. She had been given a home dialysis machine, and trained in the process of plugging it into the stent. Her renal nurse complained about the state of the house so, I suggested I could do some light cleaning. Mother gracefully allowed me to mop the floors, stock the fridge, and drag her old furniture out onto the curb.

'I need some new furniture,' she complained, so we spent a cheerful afternoon shopping. To my surprise, she bought a new sofa, curtains, and a rocking chair. After some debate, she let me buy her some rugs and a bedside table. 'I've always wanted nice new things,' she confessed.

'Did you? I thought you were committed to hard rubbish?'

'Well, you do get lots of nice things that way,' she conceded, 'but I've always wanted new things. It's just that they cost a lot more.'

By the time I returned to Sydney, the house looked very nearly clean and, for a while, everything seemed fine. Mother started dialysis, stopped having angina attacks, and seemed like her old self. Then she began feeling nauseated and quickly lost fifteen kilograms. She rang to tell me she was going on a diet. 'I'm having trouble putting on weight, so the doctors say I need to eat lots of pastries with cream. It's quite nice.'

Her doctors thought the dialysis machine was draining too much fluid out of her body. They tinkered with the volumes being pumped out and then with the volumes being pumped in. Her appetite returned but she was still underweight.

After that, something happened to her blood pressure, although I could never understand exactly what. Rather than alter the dialysis again, the doctors changed her heart medication, thinning her blood until she became foggy and light headed.

Things went on like this for months. Each time I returned to Adelaide, I found she had grown slightly smaller, although she remained on her diet of pastries and cream. I started contemplating ways to bring us back together. I dreamt of buying a house large enough for her to move to Sydney and live with us. Although I had found a full-time job, and Diana had two teaching jobs on top of her scholarship, all of our income disappeared into rent.

One hot February day, Mother phoned me from hospital. She had been pottering about on the back porch, fainted, and hit her head. 'I'm all right,' she reassured me, 'I just thought I'd let you know.'

'Do you need me to fly back?'

'No, I've just got a little bump on the back of my head.'

A week later, the bump on the back of her head hadn't healed. Instead, it morphed into a large and painful welt. She was sent back to hospital again. 'The doctors say my blood thinners have stopped my blood from clotting and the bump on my head has turned septic.'

She spent a month in hospital having skin shorn off her inner thigh and transplanted on to her scalp. On the morning she was discharged I flew back to pick her up. Diana insisted on coming with me. 'You always get so depressed when you go back to Adelaide,' she told me. 'I think you could probably use some help.'

She was right. When we picked Mother up from the hospital, she was missing all the hair on one side of her head. In its place she had a gigantic glistening slab of raw skin. That night, it developed a large blister. 'I think the skin graft might be failing,' she said.

We took her back to the hospital where the doctor on duty inspected her wound and casually pierced the blister with a long needle. He explained that the wound was healing normally but needed to be protected from the sun.

'I'm going to buy you a headscarf,' Diana told her.

'That's very kind of you dear but it's a bit hot for a head scarf. I think what I need is an ice cream.'

We went to the gift store and got her an ice cream and a headscarf. Mother accepted both, but wore the scarf in such a way as to leave the graft exposed. We stayed for a week, until she had settled back into her routine.

Soon after, Mother had another argument with Gran. I couldn't figure out what it was about as, when I called, Mother would only tell me Gran didn't understand she was a grown woman. Eventually I rang Merridy, who said she couldn't understand what they were arguing about either. 'Your grandmother told your mother she needed an emergency beacon. And you know how your mother feels about taking advice from Gran.'

A few weeks earlier, Gran had bought an emergency beacon for herself because she kept having dizzy spells. It looked like a small remote control, worn on a lanyard or kept in a pocket, which she could press if she felt faint. She accidentally triggered it quite regularly, whereupon my aunt received an automated call from an ominous voice proclaiming a grim emergency.

Mother objected to the idea. She pointed out, not without reason, that Gran never triggered it when she was having an actual emergency. There had been three occasions where she had needed an ambulance and each time the beacon was found on her bedside table or by the sofa. Its major purpose had been to induce a heightened sense of anxiety in my aunt. In this, it was extremely effective.

Mother's doctors also entered a period of debate. Her kidney doctor, who she had known for years, spent an entire morning yelling at her heart doctor. Afterwards, a small and multidisciplinary committee was formed, consisting of senior medical professionals who met every few weeks to review her blood levels, prescribe new medications, and tinker with her dialysis.

They must have done a reasonable job as her head wound healed and, much to everyone's surprise, her hair began to grow back. For several months, nothing went wrong. Mother resumed pottering about the garden and walking Arthur along the river. When I called, she would discuss the usual subjects: she had been to a house inspection and decided not to move, Gran and she had debated the merits of emergency beacons, Arthur had been put on a new arthritis medication. My family entered a brief, uneasy peace.

27

Fear and Hope – those are the names of the two great passions which rule the race of man.
— William Morris

At the start of the following year, Diana completed her thesis. 'It's not very good,' she explained, 'I'm never going to get a job.'

Three months later, it won a prestigious award, she got a job as a lecturer, and was invited to a six-month residency in London. When I told my mother, she was immensely impressed. 'That's wonderful news. Tell her I'm very proud of her. I always knew she'd do brilliantly.'

'Really?' I asked. 'You've always seemed a bit snippy with her.'

'I most certainly have not! Diana and I get on very well.'

'I'm thinking I might go with her to London. I've got some leave stored up.'

'You could go to Kew Gardens. That's a marvellous idea.'

When I passed on Mother's congratulations, Diana contemplated it for several minutes. 'You know, I think she's never quite forgiven me for stealing you away to Sydney and making you middle class. But now I'm taking you on an adventure, so I think she's a bit more forgiving.'

A week later, Mother raised the prospect of flying to London with us. There was, she said, a sort of patient exchange service offered between hospitals, so people on dialysis could take holidays. We discussed how it might work; that she would perhaps come for a week, and stay in a good hotel in the city centre where she could rest easily and visit historic sites at her leisure.

'What do your doctors think?' I asked her.

'Well, I haven't really discussed it with them yet,' she admitted.

A week later, I raised the subject again and she was evasive. 'My doctors aren't very favourable to the idea.'

'What did they actually say?'

'They aren't very favourable,' she repeated.

They did, however, concede she might visit me in Sydney. Her sixty-fifth birthday fell two months before we left for London, so we planned the trip around this auspicious occasion. In preparation, several boxes full of dialysis equipment were sent to me, and I bought a fold-out bed for her to sleep on. When Mother appeared a few days later, I was pleased to find her hair had grown back almost completely. She was still thin and pale, but she was in high spirits.

By then, Diana and I had moved to a respectable art deco apartment in one of the better parts of town. I had hoped Mother would be impressed but her reaction was ambiguous. She seemed to have filled her suitcases with sand and used tissues, which she sprinkled liberally throughout our living room. When I objected, she told me to stop being pedantic but made a vague apology to Diana.

'I know you like things to be clean,' she said, 'Personally, I don't see the point but it's your house.'

We took her on a ferry, visited the art galleries, and spent an afternoon in the botanic gardens. Diana booked us into a fancy restaurant, where Mother ate most of her mains and all of her desserts. 'I hear there's some very good museums in London?' she asked.

'Yes, there is,' Diana told her. 'Great museums and great art galleries.'

'Do you think you'll go to Kew Gardens?'

'Yes, Ianto says he wants to.'

'And there's a museum called the Victoria and Albert, with a tea room designed by William Morris. Do you like William Morris?'

'I know Ianto does.'

'I'm very glad you're taking him with you. In the past, all his girlfriends moved overseas without him. Although if they'd stayed, he might not have ended up with you, which would have been terrible.'

'I wouldn't dream of leaving him behind.'

'I think that's very kind of you,' Mother said and returned to her dessert.

She stayed for two more days, which we spent visiting historic houses and public gardens. I took her shopping, where she bought some new floral shirts and a duffel coat for the coming winter. On the night before she returned to Adelaide, I found her perched on the sofa in our living room, dipping her toe in and out of an expensive salad bowl she had filled with salted water.

Diana retreated to the kitchen. When I went to check on her, she asked, 'Why is Dimity washing her foot in our good salad bowl?'

'I'm not sure,' I told her.

'Do you think she needs to do it on our coffee table, or

could she go into the bathroom? I know she's tried very hard on this trip, but do you think you could ask her to stop?'

I returned to the living room and stood watching Mother for several minutes. She was deeply engrossed in her task, dipping her foot in and out of the salad bowl, and then placing it on the coffee table while she peered at her toes.

'Mother, why are washing your foot in our good salad bowl?'

'Well I have to wash it. My toe has gone black,' she explained.

'Why is your toe black?'

Her answer was unclear. As far as I could gather, she had banged it on something a few weeks earlier and it hadn't healed.

'Have you seen a doctor about it?'

'I have been bathing it twice a day in salt water.'

'Do you think you should see a doctor?'

'I've been bathing it twice a day,' she repeated.

'Do you need to use our good salad bowl?'

'Well, it's the right size and depth for washing a foot,' she explained. 'There's no reason you can't use it for salad again, provided you rinse it properly.'

I let the point drop. The next morning, she flew back to Adelaide and we all declared the trip a success. 'I had a lovely time,' she told us, 'I'm going to fly back again at Christmas.'

I visited Mother in Adelaide once more before I went to London. She was as cheerful as ever but her toe had grown much worse. The black spot now covered two toes and part of her foot. Her doctors said it was caused by the same arterial calcification that had caused her heart attack. The veins in her legs were so badly blocked that blood wasn't reaching her feet. She was instructed to wear a large medicinal plastic shoe, which she referred to as a moon boot.

Unexpectedly, it gave her a brief moment of unity with my grandmother, who had been instructed to wear a similar boot after breaking her toe some years earlier. 'They told her to wear it for six weeks,' Mother explained, 'but she hated it so much that, after three days, she took it off and threw it into the garden.'

The moon boot meant Mother could not drive. She had been confined to the house, so I spent most of the trip driving Arthur and her around the suburb, re-visiting their favourite parks and fish and chip shops. Arthur's arthritis was so bad he needed to be lifted in and out of the car. I drove them to the local oval and watched as they hobbled about.

Mother was cheerful as ever. 'That was very tiring, wasn't it, Arthur?' she said. 'I think we need some pancakes and cream, don't we?'

'Is he allowed to eat pancakes?'

'Karen's been taking me to a pancake restaurant in Port Adelaide. Arthur has wanted to try it for months.'

I drove them down to the pancake restaurant. It was on the docks, facing out onto the water. Port Adelaide had once been the city's primary port but it had been mostly abandoned in the seventies. The big ships all went to a new container port further down the coast and the water was empty except for a few dingy looking yachts.

Mother ordered a mound of pancakes covered in the kind of whipped cream that comes out of an aerosol can. We sat at a table gazing out over the empty wharves, grimy river, and vacant warehouses.

Across the way, I could see a gigantic, rotting hulk, surrounded by a mesh fence. 'What on earth is that?'

'It's the *City of Adelaide*.'

I thought she was joking.

'No,' she explained, 'it's the hull of a clipper, one of those old sailing ships.'

It had spent several decades slowly rotting in a wrecker's yard in Scotland until it had been loaded onto a cargo ship and brought back to South Australia at great public expense.

'Apparently, there's only two clippers left, so they're going to turn it into a museum. They think it will revive the local economy,' Mother explained.

'Is that a good idea?'

'I'm not sure', she said, chewing her pancakes. 'But the other one is in London. Maybe you can visit it and let me know?'

Later in the afternoon, we drove up to visit my grandparents. Over lunch, we told my grandfather about the hulk of the *City of Adelaide*, and he repeated the story of his father taking him to see the last of the great windjammers coming into port when he was a boy. He repeated it several times. His dementia had robbed him of most of his memories, but this one remained. We spent the better part of an hour discussing it.

Mother spent the time talking to my grandmother.

'Have you been wearing your moon boot?' Gran asked her. 'The doctors said you need to.'

'What happened to your moon boot? Is it still in the garden?'

'Probably. I think it's underneath the hydrangeas.'

I left for London a week later. While Diana endured meetings and work events, I made my way through a long list of museums, gardens, galleries, and historic houses. I saw Daniel Defoe's grave in Bunhill Fields, the former residence of Virginia Woolf in Bloomsbury, and drank at pubs once frequented by

George Orwell and P. G. Wodehouse. I went to Kew Gardens three times, had lunch in the Morris tea room at the Victoria and Albert, and spent long afternoons in the British Museum.

One morning, I caught the train to Greenwich to see the *Cutty Sark*, the lone remaining clipper alongside the *City of Adelaide*. Mother was right; it had been turned into a very nice museum, built into the embankment alongside the Thames. It was virtually deserted and I strolled the decks thinking of my grandfather, aged seven, clutching the hand of his father.

Afterwards, I walked along the river, looking across to Canary Wharf. The ship my grandfather had seen more than eighty years before had, I thought, probably passed by this very spot. It struck me that I did not know my great-grandfather's name. Had I ever known it? I thought for several seconds. No, I thought not.

Nancy Mitford once described her feeling of London as 'more literary and historic than personal' and I suppose this had been my experience. I had seen the remnants of the great and good; their graves, their houses, and those fragments they left in the various museums. Yet I remained remarkably ignorant of my own antecedents. I felt much as I had when, at age six, my class had dressed as settlers and marched around the basketball court. It was a strangely hollow sensation.

That night, I subscribed to an online ancestry website, operated by Mormons for some nefarious purpose of their own. I followed my grandfather's line back, first to my great-grandparents, and then until I found a series of shipping records for Charles and Una Ware, the last of my ancestors to pass along the Thames. They had, I found, lived in the village of Bexley, on the outer rim of Greater London, and had left for

Australia in the late 1830s.

By a stroke of fate, I already had Bexley on my itinerary. It was the location of William Morris's former home, now a museum managed by the National Trust. When I told Diana, she was not impressed. 'If I knew you were going to get into family history I would have left you at home.'

'We could catch the train out there. I think it will be interesting.'

'I think you're having a mid-life crisis.'

'You can tell my mother we went to William Morris's house. She'll be very impressed.'

In the end she came with me, although she did not enjoy it. Bexley has long been absorbed into the outer suburbs of Greater London, wedged between the A2 and the A207. We stepped out of the train station to find the old village centre jammed with cars. I had underestimated the distance to Morris's house and we spent a long hour tramping down a four-lane freeway.

'So this is the land of your ancestors,' observed Diana.

We joined two women with prams, trying to cross a roundabout through the roaring traffic, and then passed a doctor's office, with a sign reading 'Yellow Fever', before turning down a side street lined with soot-stained houses.

'I think this is the right way,' I said, although it took us another twenty minutes to reach our destination. Fortunately, the Morris house itself was beautiful, built in glowing red brick with stained glass windows. His garden was still intact, lovingly maintained, full of flowers, herbs, and fruit trees.

'It is actually quite lovely,' Diana admitted, 'Dimity would love this. We should take some photos for her.'

We took pictures of the plants, the potting shed, and the

compost pile, and purchased some Morris memorabilia from the gift shop; postcards with his wallpaper patterns and tea towels emblazoned with his wittier quotes.

I also bought a booklet on the history of Bexley to read on the trip back to London. I read most of it at the station as the train was almost an hour late, including a description of the area by the British journalist and politician William Cobbett, who travelled there in the 1820s, a few years before my ancestors left:

> The land, generally speaking... is poor and the surface ugly by nature, to which ugliness there has been made ... a considerable addition by the inclosure of a common, and by the sticking up of some shabby-genteel houses, surrounded with dead fences and things called gardens, in all manner of ridiculous forms, making, all together, the bricks, hurdle-rods and earth say, as plainly as the can speak, 'Here dwell vanity and poverty.'

As we waited, a small boy rode along the platform on his BMX, screaming obscenities. When the train finally arrived, I sat by the window, looking out at the suburbs. They looked at once familiar and unsettling.

Two weeks later, I flew back to Sydney. I called my mother. 'Bexley was a bit of a hole,' I told her. 'But William Morris's house was lovely. I took a picture of his potting shed and bought you a couple of tea towels.'

'That's nice dear.'

'And I visited the *Cutty Sark*.'

'The what?'

'The clipper ship, like the *City of Adelaide*. It was a good museum, but there was no one there.'

'Oh, that's a shame.'

'Do you think you'll still come and visit us at Christmas?'

'I don't think so dear.'

'Why not?'

She seemed distracted and changed the subject. When I pressed the point, she admitted she could no longer walk. Although she had diligently worn the moon boot, her blackened toe had failed to heal. Instead, it had rotted down to the bone. Black marks had spread up her calf. Her veins were so badly calcified her doctors said they would need to amputate her leg at the knee.

'I'm sorry dear,' she said, 'but I'm going to have to sell the house. They say I need to buy a spot in an aged care home.'

She had spoken to a real estate agent, who had already found a prospective buyer. He would, they said, demolish the place, clear the block, and install two cube houses. I booked a flight to Adelaide to help her prepare.

28

You do not die from being born, nor from having lived, nor from old age. You die from something.
— Simone de Beauvoir

When I look back on the final months of my mother's life, I can see a definite downward trajectory. This was not clear at the time. Instead, we lumbered along as if lost in a heavy gale, unable to see the path ahead. I spent that first trip back to Adelaide driving between various aged care villages with her and Merridy, discussing the future.

'I intend to live until I'm eighty,' Mother reminded me.

She had found a unit with a small courtyard garden and good natural light. She talked us through the various planter beds and hanging plants she intended to install. 'I've got a good price for the house, so I'll be able to move somewhere nice. And I won't have to move out for six months, so I don't have to rush.'

Shortly after I returned to Sydney, Arthur died. It was not unexpected as he was old, fat, and his arthritis had rendered him incapable of walking more than a few steps.

Mother rang me after he had been euthanized. 'The vet came to the house to give him the injection,' she told me. 'They said he was very brave.'

I called her a few days later and the phone was answered by an ambulance driver. 'Sorry mate, your mum's had a bit of a fall.'

He handed over the phone and Mother's voice reassured me, 'I'm fine. I just had a bit of a slip.'

I flew back to Adelaide again. By the time I arrived, she had been discharged with a huge bruise running from her chin to her forehead, and a deep gash across her nose. It was hard to extract an explanation of what had happened, only that she had tripped on something and my aunt was somehow to blame.

I inspected the spot by her bed where she had fallen. It was marked by a patch of dried blood and a small, crumpled throw rug.

'Did you put this throw rug here?'

'Yes.'

'Do you think this is what you tripped on?'

'No.'

'But isn't this where you fell over?'

'I let Merridy do some cleaning last week, and she moved everything around,' Mother assured me. 'I would have been fine otherwise.'

Her doctors gave her a walking frame, and she shuffled cheerfully about the house, telling me which plants she intended to take with her, and which she had promised to her friends. She calculated that, after selling her house and buying the unit, she would have enough money to buy herself some nice furniture. I took her to visit some designer furniture stores, where she inspected Danish sofas and Marimekko curtains. 'I know I'm decaying, and I intend to decay as comfortably as possible,' she told me.

We spent the trip talking about the move. Her house contained three decades worth of clutter, old furniture, and the various objects d'art she had acquired from the local op shops and hard rubbish. In the mornings, I piled these into the bin or put them back on the curb. In the afternoons, I took her out to inspect furniture stores, where she hobbled between brightly coloured arm chairs and bed spreads. We found an oak leaf patterned fabric she liked, and priced turning it into curtains.

On the last day of my visit, we returned from our shopping trip to find someone had smashed open one of the back windows. They hadn't stolen anything, just rifled through her cupboards and wardrobe. We phoned the police. As nothing had been stolen, they were not particularly interested.

Two officers turned up and wandered through the house for a while. 'They were probably looking for drugs,' said one.

'Yes, they either mistook your house for the drug dealer next door, or they saw the district nurse visiting and thought you might be getting morphine.'

That night, I sat on the foot of Mother's bed while she plugged herself into the tubes of the dialysis machine. Together, we watched the bags of clear fluid drain in and out of her stomach.

'Are you still planning to live to eighty?'

'Oh, of course. I might not have the standard of living I wanted but you don't need to worry.'

I don't know why I believed her. When I finally settled down on the sofa bed in the spare room, I could hear her coughing, and then the irregular grumble as she started to snore. This would be the last time we stayed in the house together.

A week later she fell over again. At the time I thought this was simply a misfortune, yet it was the trigger for the downward spiral of the following two months. The fall damaged a muscle in her arm and it would not heal. After that, she caught her finger on the handle of her walking frame, it turned black, and then became infected. She was kept in hospital while it was amputated.

During the operation, she remained awake, with her arm concealed by a curtain behind which the surgical staff operated, chatting happily with her as they sawed off her finger. 'The anaesthetist kept apologising for the background music,' she told me. 'They were playing someone called Ed Sheeran. Apparently, the head surgeon liked him, and the head surgeon gets to pick the music. All the others hated it.'

After the operation, her finger was spirited away, never to be seen again, and she was sent back to the renal ward to recoup. The following week, the stump of her finger was still infected and would not heal. She was kept in hospital while her doctors reviewed and altered her medication. When I visited again, she was still too ill to return home.

I stayed in the house alone. In her absence, the garden had become strangely barren. The oaks still loomed over the house, and the light still filtered through their leaves as it had when Tubby and I had done our rounds, but it no longer felt as it once had. It was autumn, and the trees had lost their leaves. The summer heat had killed off most of the undergrowth and the smaller shrubs and, without Mother there to water and replant, everything had withered away.

With the settlement date looming, I spent my days dragging her furniture out into the driveway, smashing it up with a sledgehammer, and piling it into a gigantic metal bin. Most of it was the furniture I had grown up with, dragged from hard rubbish years ago, and irrevocably worn and battered. None of it was worth keeping, or even in good enough condition to take to the charity store at the local shopping centre.

In the evenings, I visited Mother in hospital, where she showed me the stump of her finger, wrapped in bandages. 'I suppose it makes me a bit sad,' she admitted, 'I'll never see the soil under my nail again.'

On the last night, alone in the spare room, I found myself feeling unsafe, as if someone might walk in at any moment. It was a feeling I had not experienced since boyhood, when, after school in the short winter days, I waited for Mother to return from work. I remembered when it grew dark, and I would hide in the hallway, convinced someone was lurking outside. In the morning, I woke up thinking about her leg and its impending amputation.

Over the following weeks, the small parliament of Mother's doctors met with increased regularity. They decided she was too weak for a prosthetic and would need a motorised wheel chair. The unit she had chosen was deemed unsuitable for such a device, and the only alternative was far more expensive, meaning she would have no money left over for her new furniture after all.

As an added insult, she was told she needed to have her cat, Dharma, put down as the new place did not allow pets. 'I wanted to re-house her,' she explained, 'but the vet said she was too old and too vicious. They said it would have been cruel.'

A date was set for the removal of her leg, although her finger had not yet healed and she remained in hospital. At one point, she rallied her energies for one last major argument with my grandmother, who was in another hospital having had one of her fainting episodes.

Fortunately, the conflict ended as quickly as it had begun, not because it reached some resolution but because both of them recognised it was pointless. Neither of them apologised. I think they simply accepted that whatever they'd been fighting over for the past sixty years was no longer a subject of debate.

Mother was transferred to a respite centre, where we assumed she would stay until the sale of the house was finalised and she moved into the aged care unit. I rang her after her first night and she muttered something about her dialysis which I couldn't understand. Later that evening she was transferred into intensive care as she had become delusional. She remained in this state for the better part of two weeks.

During most of this time, my aunt stayed with her. When Mother regained her senses, she was transferred out of intensive care and back into the renal unit. She called upon the counsel of her various doctors and a few favoured nurses. It was early May, and the weather had begun to shift from autumnal to wintery.

They came to visit her one by one over the course of a day, each consulting the latest charts and test results. Her options, she concluded, were limited. At best, she might limp on, living in hospital or aged care, for a year or two. At worst, she would not recover from the amputation of her leg. Her doctors conceded they were not sure she would survive the operation. Overnight, she decided that she no longer wished to live. In the morning, she told the doctors she wanted to cease all of her treatments. She rang me the following morning and I booked a flight for that afternoon.

When I arrived, I found her sitting in the hospital bed with my grandmother perched on a stool behind her. I stayed in the hospital with her that night and, the next morning, an ambulance transported us from the hospital's renal unit over to the hospice.

As they prepared for her transfer, she discussed the coming days with her favourite nurse. 'How long will this take?' she asked.

'How long do you want?'

She thought about it for a few minutes. 'I think a week should do.'

'Don't underestimate the power of your own will in these things,' the nurse advised her.

With this, Mother was loaded into the ambulance, where I sat beside her sobbing. At the hospice, she was wheeled into a small room facing onto a tiny garden and we sat for some minutes alone.

'This isn't living,' she told me, 'I hope you understand.'

'I understand your decision. You don't need to justify it.'

'I'm sorry dear. I know you need your mother.'

'I don't need you, I just would have liked another twenty years.' I had read that those about to die often need reassurance their loved ones will survive without them, yet she looked disappointed.

She grew progressively calmer over the following days. For the first time in forty years, all of her innumerable medications had been ceased and she was placed on a steady diet of pain killers. Neither the stump of her finger nor her rotten feet seemed to bother her. Kidney failure, the actual cause of her death, appeared to cause no pain at all. On her first night in the hospice she was given some laxatives and produced a turd so immense the nurses placed it in a plastic bag and paraded it around the ward showing it to their colleagues. After that, she began to sleep for longer and longer periods.

When she was awake, we would talk until she fell asleep again. I reminded her of the time she saw the Virgin Mary. 'You're not experiencing any death bed conversions?' I asked.

'No, I don't think I need them.'

She specified she wanted a 'natural' burial, at a cemetery where the graves were left unmarked by headstones and slowly absorbed back into bushland.

Otherwise, she offered no instructions for the ceremony. Over the following days, she cried a little when saying goodbye to friends and family but seemed surprisingly unperturbed.

On the last night, a week after we'd entered the hospice, I settled into the recliner next to her and held her hand. I could not sleep but she began to snore deeply. About one in the morning, it became clear she was no longer breathing, and that was the end of it.

I only went back to the house once after she died. There, on her bedside table, I found a poem she'd written on the back of an old envelope:

> Death is not a large hooded
> Scythe carrying vision.
> It doesn't come dashing out of
> The night.
> It's just there.

I walked back out onto the street. The weather was dry, but bitterly cold, with clouds of dead leaves chattering along the pavement in the wind.

29

We are the background to history.
— Sheila Rowbotham

In the early stages of mourning, there's a tendency to assume death is the defining event in one's relationship to the deceased. Grief is, I think, a sort of shock, and I spent the months after Mother's death in a state of bewildered exhaustion, unable to think of anything beyond her dying.

My aunt and I organised the funeral, with Diana's help. My grandmother arrived bristling for a fight, and remained so for much of the ceremony. Eventually Gran admitted that she was angry her daughter was dead and had, at some subconscious level, turned up ready to argue the point. Finding Mother unable to reciprocate, she seemed at a loss.

The director of the funeral company spent most of the ceremony trying to read out his own poetic compositions, and I spent much of it trying to stop him. I had asked Diana to give the eulogy, and afterwards the casket was taken out to a muddy hole in the near-by scrub for burial. The grave, unmarked would slowly be reclaimed by the bush until no marker but the trees remained to recall the location of Mother's body.

The next morning, I signed the last of the papers associated with the sale of the house and returned to Sydney. A few weeks later, Merridy phoned to say the developers had knocked it down, cut down all the trees, and cleared the block.

By spring, I had recovered my wits enough to contemplate my mother's legacy, as distinct from her death. I had unexpectedly inherited the value of the house and her unused superannuation, which I used to buy an apartment for Diana and I in the nicest part of Sydney, on a hill above the harbour. Now, each November, as I walk through the surrounding streets, I encounter avenues of jacaranda, blooming purple against the blue sky, and I think of those days after Mother's transplant — when she first fell for June the hypochondriac, and tapped the wellspring that made her the person I knew.

My mother was not one of history's famous men but, like so many good and deserving people, she dragged the world along behind her. Of course, the vast majority of good and deserving people go unremembered, and our histories are too often left to the monopoly of those rich and famous enough to write them. Yet even in this age, with all its stupid indifference to the past, an outstanding personality might still win an occasional triumph. Here, I have told my mother's story to posterity, and by that she will live.